Legal Issues in
the Care of
Psychiatric Patients

Robert L. Sadoff, M.D., is Clinical Professor of Psychiatry and Director of the Center for Studies in Social Legal Psychiatry at the University of Pennsylvania, and Lecturer in Law at Villanova University School of Law. He is the author of three other books, including *Forensic Psychiatry: A Practical Guide for Lawyers and Psychiatrists*. He has served as president of the American Academy of Psychiatry and the Law. He has also served on a number of commissions, task forces, and committees of the American Bar Association, where he is currently a member of the Commission on the Mentally Disabled. In addition, he is chairman of the Guttmacher Award Board of the American Psychiatric Association. He has worked on other committees writing model mental health legislation, and has authored over 70 articles in professional journals and over a dozen chapters in books on psychiatry and law. He has lectured throughout the United States and in Canada, England, Ireland, Israel, and Greece.

Legal Issues in the Care of Psychiatric Patients

A Guide for the Mental Health Professional

Robert L. Sadoff, M.D.

Foreword by Michael L. Perlin, J.D.

Springer Publishing Company

New York

Springer Publishing Company, Inc.
200 Park Avenue South
New York, New York 10003

82 83 84 85 86 / 10 9 8 7 6 5 4 3 2 1

Library of Congress Cataloging in Publication Data

Sadoff, Robert L.
  Legal issues in the care of psychiatric patients.

  Bibliography: p.
  Includes index.
  1. Forensic psychiatry.   2. Mental health
laws.   I. Title.   [DNLM: 1. Forensic psychiatry—
United States—Legislation.   2. Psychiatry—United
States—Legislation.   WM 33 AA1 S24L]
RA1151.S23   1982   344.73'044   82-5946
ISBN 0-8261-3650-8   347.3044   AACR2
ISBN 0-8261-3651-6 (pbk.)

Printed in the United States of America

To all mental health professionals who have agonized through the confusion of the changes in the law that affect our practice; and to the patients who may benefit only from such changes that are designed to provide quality mental health care with the highest respect for personal integrity, liberty, and mental health.

Contents

Foreword

It is doubtful that any area of the law has developed as rapidly or as completely in the past decade as has mental health law. Cases have been decided by state and federal courts, and statutes have been enacted with dizzying speed by the U.S. Congress and by state legislatures. As a result of this recent flurry, it has become essential that mental health practitioners begin to familiarize themselves with legal concepts and trends in the law so that they can assimilate these changes and make use of them in their daily practice.

The courts do not expect mental health practitioners to be lawyers, but they do expect professionals to understand the legal system and its role in the regulation of mental health practice. To this end, practitioners must become sensitive to legal principles, rights, and responsibilities and to the full impact of the law on the delivery of mental health services.

I can think of no finer way for such practitioners to familiarize themselves with these concepts than to read Robert Sadoff's new book, *Legal Issues in the Care of Psychiatric Patients: A Guide for the Mental Health Professional*. In this one volume, Dr. Sadoff has accomplished what might appear at first blush to be impossible: He has written a readable, coherent, up-to-date, provocative treatise on virtually every relevant area of mental health law, a book that will be of value to the full range of mental health practitioners.

The work encompasses both contemporary and traditional problems in all areas of the civil and criminal law. It analyzes the difficult problem of the right to refuse treatment, the anxiety-provoking issue of malpractice, and the sometimes puzzling area of developing constitutional rights of patients. Although the book has a clear point of view, it is never polemical; it is balanced without traditional psychiatric bias. It prods the reader into thinking— seriously—about the serious problems under discussion. Most important, it is clear and cohesive; unlike many other supposedly scholarly tomes, it can be read and understood easily.

Dr. Sadoff is a preeminent forensic psychiatrist, a gifted therapist, a skilled lecturer and teacher, and a superb expert witness. This work combines the best of all of these talents.

Michael L. Perlin, J.D.
Director, Division of Mental Health Advocacy
State of New Jersey

Acknowledgments

The preparation of a book of this type necessarily must reflect the experiences the author has had in working with a number of other professionals from varied professional backgrounds who have contributed to the experiences and to the text. I am grateful to my patients, who have provided me with the clinical material that is shared in this volume. I also am grateful to my teachers in psychiatry, my colleagues in forensic psychiatry and psychology, and specifically to mental health attorneys all of whom have taught me so much about the law and mental health professions.

First and foremost, I am grateful to Michael Perlin, mental health advocate for New Jersey, with whom I have worked so closely this past decade. His contribution to the content of this book is reflected not only in his words in the foreword but also in the formulation of my thoughts, my ideas, and my experiences in this very complicated and growing field. To Dr. Jonas Rappeport, eminent forensic psychiatrist, I am grateful for continued support and encouragement, especially in the area of ethics in forensic psychiatry. His efforts have significantly influenced my thinking. Other members of the American Academy of Psychiatry and the Law with whom I have worked, debated, and discussed these issues also are gratefully acknowledged. To Dr. Gerald Cooke, a prominent forensic psychologist with whom I have worked closely during the past decade and who has contributed much to my understanding of the work in forensic psychology, I also am deeply grateful. I acknowledge gratitude to my friends and colleagues who have influenced my thinking, but I assume full responsibility for all opinions expressed in this volume.

I am deeply indebted to my fantastic secretary, Mrs. Roberta Evantash, for her skill in preparing the manuscript and her diligence in working late to complete it.

To the editors and publisher at Springer, I give thanks and credit for the superb handling, editing, and management of this book. Their suggestions for improving the original manuscript are reflected in the final product.

Finally, I am always profoundly indebted and sincerely grateful to my parents, Rose and Max Sadoff, for their lifelong support and encouragement, and to my loving wife, Joan, and my precious children, Debra, David, Julie, and Sherry, who have given up time that might have been spent with me in order that I might spend the many hours necessary for writing, rewriting, and preparing this book. They have been most generous.

Introduction

The treatment of the mentally ill has been relatively unregulated until recently. The mentally ill usually were placed in hospitals far from urban centers and benignly neglected and occasionally abused. They had few rights and even fewer remedies. Many died in the state hospitals to which they were sent, and others were abandoned by family and friends. As more humane treatment of the mentally ill emerged, it was accomplished primarily by the voluntary efforts of concerned citizens and humanistic hospital superintendents. Nevertheless, abuses abounded and many patients committed to state hospitals were mistreated and unrepresented in the outside world. Progress in the treatment of the mentally ill came slowly and unevenly.

It was not until the mid twentieth century that widespread concern for the rights of patients was noted. Patients' rights became the hue and cry of mental health attorneys who specialized in representing the interests of the mentally ill and mentally retarded. Through lawsuits and class-action litigation, the rights of patients have become recognized and enforced. Changes in commitment proceedings and in treatment procedures within hospitals and in communities were mandated. No longer was the treatment of the mentally ill an unregulated phenomenon. No longer were mentally ill patients disenfranchised; in many states they had advocates appointed and assigned as the guardians of their civil rights.

With the abundance of regulations came the need for understanding and modification of treatment by such mental health professionals as psychiatrists, psychologists, social workers, psychiatric nurses, and all others associated with the treatment of the mentally ill and mentally retarded. This book is an attempt to acquaint mental health professionals with the changes in law that affect their practice. What are the regulations that they need to know in order to care properly for their patients and not to abuse their civil rights? When should a patient be medicated, and when should the medication be discontinued? What should be put in the records about a particular patient, and when may that information be disclosed to others? What are the rights of the mental health professional within the context of patients' rights? Where are these changes leading, and what may we expect in the future?

These and other questions will be addressed in this practical guide for the mental health professional. The book is written in such a way as to be read easily and utilized by mental health professionals of all types, especially those involved in the direct and immediate care of the mentally ill. Relevant cases will be cited, but only as background to aid in fully understanding the changes that have occurred. The major focus of this presentation will be the practical approach for those professionals who need to know what changes have occurred and how they affect our work.

During the past two decades there has been a significant increase in the publication of books and articles in forensic psychiatry, that subspecialty of psychiatry which deals with legal issues, laws, and regulations that affect the care and treatment of psychiatric patients. Especially since 1960, with the publication of Birnbaum's seminal article on psychiatric patients' rights to treatment, courts and legislatures have modified the laws that regulate the practice of psychiatrists and other mental health professionals. These rules include those governing involuntary commitment to psychiatric hospitals and patients' rights to adequate treatment, to refuse treatment, to open communication, to privacy, to confidentiality, and to freedom from coercive treatment. Patients' rights with reference to outpatient treatment and care in the community also have been addressed and protected recently.

In addition to the changes in laws and regulations that affect the practice of psychiatry and community mental health centers, there have been several major events that have helped shape the role psychiatry has played in legal issues and in courts. The first occurred in Washington, D.C. in 1954, when Judge David Bazelon promulgated the Durham decision as the test for insanity in criminal law (*United States* v. *Durham*, 1954). That decision opened the door to more complete and more meaningful psychiatric testimony in criminal cases. Modifications of the insanity test occurred in the early 1960s, including changes in the American Law Institute Model Penal Code (1962) that further refined and defined the role psychiatry could play in the utilization and presentation of the insanity defense.

Traditionally, psychiatrists and mental health experts have been involved in the criminal law with regard to the defendant's competency to stand trial and the issue of criminal responsibility. Lately there has been great controversy expressed about both issues, and laws have been passed to modify the legal definitions of competency and insanity. Other areas of concern for psychiatrists and mental health professionals working in the criminal law include the competency of the defendant to give a confession, to plead guilty, to serve time in a penitentiary, and to be executed.

Psychiatrists also are called frequently to examine and treat individuals who have been charged with crimes of passion, including homicide, sexual crimes, and arson, and to examine juveniles charged with crimes to determine whether they should be tried as juveniles or as adults. During the past two decades, the laws in most states have expanded the roles of psychiatrists in the criminal law to include testifying to such issues as diminished responsibility, determination of specific intent, and evaluation of dangerousness. Mentally deviated sex offenders and sexually dangerous persons also have been added to the list of those whom the judicial system calls upon mental health professionals to examine and to treat. An emerging area in criminal law is the growing need for treatment services for mentally ill persons confined to detention centers, jails, and prisons. Finally, questions of amnesia and the use of hypnosis and sodium amytal have arisen and have been addressed by legislators and courts.

Forensic psychiatry more recently has concerned itself increasingly with matters of civil law. Certainly the changes in regulating the treatment of the mentally ill have contributed significantly to this shift in focus; however, two other major events helped influence psychiatric thinking in civil law. One is the case of *Carter* v. *General Motors* (1960) in Michigan, which opened wide the door for psychiatric testimony in personal injury cases where an individual may suffer a traumatic psychiatric illness that is caused by psychological stress without physical injury. Personal injury matters involve a number of complex interactions that need proper assessment by psychiatrists, psychologists, and others. Individuals may be injured by accident or by others' wrong doing; they may be dealing with injuries at work or through malpractice in professional treatment matters. The emotional ramifications and consequences of such injuries and the resultant psychiatric diagnoses require identification and proper treatment. Workers' Compensation matters, Social Security Disability claims, and Disabled Veterans' claims require careful evaluation and examination in order to clarify and understand the relationship between injury, illness, and disability.

The second major event that has altered forensic psychiatry is the publication by Goldstein, Freud, & Solnit of their book, *Beyond the Best Interests of the Child* (1973), which further demonstrates the need for careful psychiatric and psychological evaluation in domestic relations matters, particularly child custody. Forensic psychiatrists and child psychiatrists have become increasingly involved in aiding courts in determination of child-custody issues and visitation procedures in divorce and annulment cases. This role is critical to the futures of many children, as well as to preventive mental health.

The area of competency in civil matters has emerged as a significant issue for forensic psychiatry. Competency to write a will, known as testamentary capacity, has long been an area of concern for forensic psychiatrists. Other areas for determination of civil competency include competency to manage one's own affairs, to get married, to enter into a contract, to testify in court, and, most recently, to make determinations about one's own treatment. This last has been acknowledged as an important issue in liaison or consultative psychiatry. Often the psychiatrist is called upon by surgeons or internists to evaluate a patient who requires a procedure that she or he is unwilling to have performed, even though it may be life saving. The psychiatrist is asked to determine whether the patient is competent to make such a decision; if not, a guardian is appointed by the court after adjudication of incompetency. However, the acceptance of such concepts as "dying with dignity" allows patients who are competent to make decisions about treatment even at the risk of their lives. This consideration is linked directly to the competent patient's right to decide to refuse medication or treatment in psychiatry.

The growth of the field of forensic psychiatry is reflected in the expansion of training programs in law and psychiatry and law and psychology, the inclusion of legal principles in medical-school education, and the rise of professional organizations devoted to these issues. The American Academy of Psychiatry and the Law was born in 1968 with eight members and currently has a membership nearing 800. The American Psychology Law Society also has developed within the past decade. The American Board of Forensic Psychiatry and the American Board of Forensic Psychology, initiated in the late 1970s, acknowledged the subspecialization of this rapidly growing field by certifying individuals who have passed rigorous tests and demonstrated substantial experience in legal psychology or forensic psychiatry.

A number of excellent textbooks have been published recently to provide in-depth and comprehensive information in the field of law, psychiatry, and mental health. The early pioneers include Bromberg, Davidson, Diamond, Guttmacher, Roche, and Weihofen. Currently, Brooks, Halleck, McGarry, Rappeport, Robitscher, Roth, Slovenko, Stone, and others continue the tradition. (Works authored by these individuals are listed in the appendix.) In addition to fine texts and monographs, there also exist several journals in legal psychiatry that have emerged in the past two decades. Perhaps the most informative and comprehensive is the *Bulletin of the American Academy of Psychiatry and the Law*, initially edited by Thomas, currently by Rada; also the *Journal of Psychiatry and Law*, edited by Epstein & Nashel, publishes important contributions to the field.

With all the books and articles written recently in legal psychiatry, why the need for the present volume? The purpose of this book is to broaden the base of readership in this rapidly growing field that affects not only psychiatrists and psychologists but also clinical social workers, psychiatric nurses, mental health professionals, and others who treat the mentally ill. The issues that have developed within the field of legal psychiatry affect all who work with psychiatric patients. Most previous publications have been written for medical students, psychiatric residents, and practitioners of psychiatry or psychology. Few have addressed the essential practical issues that the clinician, the psychiatric nurse, and other professionals must know in order to care properly for the mentally ill patient.

The scope of this presentation is intended to be comprehensive but not of great depth. Issues will be addressed and discussed, and the reader will be referred to other sources for further exploration and investigation of particular subjects. The rapid changes in the field make some of the rules obsolete as soon as they are published. It is very difficult to remain current when change is so rapid, but the tide and the direction of change will be discussed, as well as future implications for the practitioner.

A major section of the book will be devoted to the questions that practitioners have raised with regard to the changes in law that affect their practice. These include patients' rights, involuntary commitment, right to refuse treatment, confidentiality, privileged communications, privacy, informed consent, and malpractice considerations. A chapter on the rights of treaters is included as well as one on record keeping in mental health facilities. The management of the psychiatric emergency also is discussed. Finally, the book will end with a section on proposed changes for the future and recommendations to the practitioner for treatment of mentally ill individuals in the community. The book will focus at all times on the legal role of practitioners within the context of their treatment obligations.

One of the major functions of this book is to allow practitioners to be more comfortable with the newer laws that affect and regulate their practices, whether they be in psychiatry, psychology, nursing, or social work. The major legal concerns that have involved the clinicians are reflected in these pages, with practical guidelines included to help resolve apparent conflicts and to raise further questions. The intention is not to delve deeply into any one particular area but rather to help the clinician deal more effectively with the relevant concerns that have been raised by the changes in mental health law. For more complicated or complex issues and for further discussion, the reader is directed to consult an attorney, a forensic psychiatrist, or the list of suggested readings in the appendix at the end of the book.

References

American Law Institute Model Penal Code, Section 4.01, Office Draft, May 4, 1962, p. 66.

Birnbaum, M. The Right to Treatment. *American Bar Association Journal, 46,* May 1960, 499–505.

Carter v. General Motors. 361 Mich. 577, 106NW 2d 105, 1960.

Epstein, G. N. (Ed.). *The Journal of Psychiatry and Law.* New York, N.Y.: Federal Legal Publications.

Goldstein, J., Freud, A., & Solnit, A. J. *Beyond the Best Interests of the Child.* New York, N.Y.: The Free Press, 1973.

Thomas, H. E. (Ed.). *Bulletin of the American Academy of Psychiatry and the Law.* Pittsburgh, Pa.: University of Pittsburgh School of Law.

United States v. Durham. 214 F. 2d 862, 1954.

PART I

The Legal Regulation of Mental Health Practice

Chapter 1

Mental Health Professional–Patient Relationships

The relationship between a patient and a mental health professional (including psychiatrist, psychologist, psychiatric social worker, psychiatric nurse, mental health aide) may be defined as a fiduciary relationship—one involving trust. There is a duty on the part of the mental health professional to uphold the trust of the patient with respect to communications and to do no harm to the patient. These concepts originate in medical ethics but are applicable to all mental health professionals.

Confidentiality

One of the most important considerations in the relationship is that of *confidentiality*. This is an ethical matter that prohibits the professional from disclosing information, without the patient's informed consent, that has been learned in the course of working with the patient. If confidentiality is breached and damage to the patient results as a direct consequence of the improper disclosure of information, the mental health professional releasing the information may be sued by the patient. The person with the duty to the patient assumes all responsibility for maintaining this confidentiality; that is, if information about a patient is disclosed by a psychiatrist's secretary, the patient may sue the psychiatrist for failure to instruct the employee properly about confidentiality and withholding of information. This is known in the law as an *agency relationship*. Such agency relationships also may occur within hospital settings between and among members of a treatment team. In the operating room the surgeon is considered to be in charge, while others act as helpers. If any error in judgment is made leading to damage to the patient, it is the surgeon who has final responsibility. Some cynics have noted that the theory goes beyond agency and more toward the "deep pockets" philosophy; that is, the surgeon may have the greatest amount of malpractice insurance, so it would be far more productive for the plaintiff's attorney to sue the surgeon to recover significant amounts rather than a secretary or a nurse who may have no significant personal assets and no malpractice insurance.

This concept is especially important in hospital settings where teams of individuals treat patients together and individually. The treatment team usually consists of a psychiatrist; psychologist; social worker; psychiatric nurse; occupational, music, art, or recreational therapists; and psychiatric aides. Conferences are held on a regular basis to discuss the patient, and each mental health professional has an opportunity to work with the patient and report back to the team. Within the team concept, confidentiality is often confusing. Patients may request a particular member of the team not to disclose specific information to other members of the team. This kind of request, if followed, may serve to disrupt the unity of the team approach and cause a rift between and among team members. This splitting of the team never can be in the best interest of the patient, and team members should be advised that secrecy should not occur among the team members; rather, the team should keep information confidential from others not in direct care of the patient. If a particular mental health professional is asked to withhold information from other members of the team by the patient, the proper response is that secrecy cannot be guaranteed and perhaps the patient should not disclose the information to the team member if unwilling to share that information with all members of the team treating the patient.

Patients sometimes attempt to manipulate others in the hospital by disclosing information and then asking that it be kept secret and not recorded in the chart. At times they may do this with different members of the team, attempting to ingratiate themselves to particular individuals. One often may view the psychodynamics of the patient–staff relationship as likely to be similar to the patient's intrafamilial interactions.

Information shared within the team meetings need not always be placed on the patient's record if that information is inflammatory, unproven, or speculative.

A particular problem may exist in group psychotherapy, wherein patients themselves are asked to maintain the confidentiality of the disclosures of other patients. There is no guarantee this will occur, and the group therapist must acknowledge at the outset the possibility of leaks of information.

When the psychiatrist consults another doctor or mental health professional to help treat the patient, she should tell the patient who the consultant is, for what purpose she is called, and that she must share information with her. In effect, the consultant becomes part of the treatment team and also assumes responsibility for maintaining confidentiality.

In summary, confidentiality is an ethical matter that must be upheld as part of the duty of the mental health professional to the patient. An inappropriate breach of this duty may lead to damage to the patient and a resultant lawsuit against the mental health professional and/or the hospital.

The ethics of the American Medical Association (1973) regarding confidentiality, which affect all professional–patient relationships, are best paraphrased as follows: "A physician may not reveal the confidences entrusted to him in the course of medical attendance, or the deficiencies he may observe in the character of patients, unless he is required to do so by law or unless it becomes necessary in order to protect the welfare of the individual or of the community."

The interpretation of this statement has led to some confusion among practitioners. It is clear there is no rule of absolute secrecy with respect to information about a patient. If the patient is imminently suicidal or violent toward others, the mental health professional, notably the psychiatrist in this instance, has the obligation to breach confidentiality in order to protect the life of the patient or the life or health of a third party. This interpretation has been upheld recently in two notable cases, *Tarasoff* v. *The Regents of the University of California* (1974) and *McIntosh* v. *Milano* (1979). In both cases the court identified a specific duty on the part of the clinician to warn the intended victim of the patient's stated violent intentions. Confidentiality is necessary for effective psychiatric treatment; however, a guarantee of secrecy may lead to a manipulation of the therapeutic relationship that may be devastating and ultimately disruptive of the therapeutic alliance.

Applying the ethics statement of the American Medical Association to psychiatrists, the American Psychiatric Association (1973) is on record for the following statement:

> A psychiatrist may release confidential information only with the authorization of the patient or under proper legal compulsion. . . . This may become an issue when the patient is being investigated by a government agency, is applying for a position, or is involved in a legal action. . . . Ethically the psychiatrist may disclose only that information which is immediately relevant to a given situation. [p. 1063]

The ethics affecting the practice of psychiatry also include the practice of psychology, psychiatric nursing, social work, and other mental health professions.

With respect to court mandate or court order to reveal information, the mental health professional may use discretion in either complying with the order or dissenting within the structure of the law. The professional should have the right to question whether there is adequate need for disclosure of information and to request the right to disclose only that information which is particularly relevant to the legal question involved.

In sum, the ethical duty is to maintain a therapeutic attitude and a therapeutic relationship as long as possible. When breaching confidentiality disrupts an otherwise intact therapeutic alliance, unless there is an emergency, the information should not be disclosed. There are times, however, when *failure* to disclose will lead to disruption of the therapeutic relationship and possible injury or death to the patient or someone else. At those times, in order to preserve the life or health of others or the therapeutic relationship, the information may be disclosed. Within a hospital or clinical setting, it may be preferable to consult a respected colleague before disclosing information or to determine legally if disclosure is necessary.

Privilege and the Right to Privacy

People often confuse confidentiality with privilege and with the right to privacy. Within the legal framework of treatment, these issues are separate and must be differentiated clearly.

Privilege, as opposed to confidentiality, is a legal matter written into the statutes. Privilege may differ among various jurisdictions and also may vary from one mental health professional to another. For example, in Pennsylvania, the psychiatrist works under the "physician–patient privilege," a fairly limited constraint that may boil down to whether or not the physician, testifying about her patient, would tend to "blacken the character" of the patient by her testimony. There are so many automatic waivers of privilege that one cannot count on being able to withhold testimony under the physician–patient privilege. The privilege belongs to the patient, not to the mental health professional. Basically, the privilege is that of the patient to keep his treater from testifying against him in a court of law. In the following exceptions, however, the treater may assume that privilege is inoperant.

1. The patient is not in treatment but was an examinee at the request of the judge or attorney, for legal purposes.
2. In the event the patient becomes involved in a criminal matter, he automatically waives his privilege of the doctor's silence.
3. If the patient raises the issue of his mental state in a civil action in order to gain an award from the court (either money damages in a personal injury suit or visitation or custody privileges in a domestic relations matter), he has waived his privilege of the treater's silence in court.

In Pennsylvania, by contrast to the physician–patient privilege, a psychologist has a privileged relationship with her client that is equal to that of the attorney–client privilege. Thus, the patient who is treated by a clinical psychologist in Pennsylvania has a stronger privilege in court than does a patient who is treated by a psychiatrist.

Some states have introduced psychotherapist–patient privilege statutes free of the encumbrances of physician–patient privilege and as strong as attorney–client privilege. In these cases, the definition of psychotherapist becomes extremely important; particular professionals are listed in the state as qualified "psychotherapists" for this privilege. Privilege mostly affects the one-on-one relationship and may be waived in the event of group psychotherapy, family therapy, or where there are more than two people in the room sharing information that might be considered privileged.

In sum, the privilege belongs to the patient and may be invoked to keep the treater from testifying against the patient. If the judge rules there is a privilege, then the therapist is precluded from testifying against a patient about what was learned in the course of treating the patient.

The third concept is that of *privacy*. Recently, courts have upheld the patient's right to privacy, which has been differentiated from the patient's privilege and the doctor's ethical duty of confidentiality. Obviously all three are interrelated in order to protect the communications of the patient in the course of therapy; however, the patient's right to privacy may have implications reaching far beyond confidentiality and privilege.

In a recent case in Pennsylvania (*In Re B*, 1977) the Supreme Court upheld a patient's right not to allow her medical records to be ordered into court in the adjudication of her son. The court noted the patient was not a party to the litigation and had a right to the privacy of her medical records, which were not necessary or essential in achieving proper adjudication of her son's case. A reasonable alternative plan of evaluation was proposed but rejected by the lower court. The Supreme Court saw fit to accept that plan as an alternative to breaching the privacy of the patient through examining her prior medical records.

Recent cases involving the patient's right to treatment and right to refuse treatment have hinged on the patient's right to the privacy of his thought processes. One cannot intrude upon the private thoughts of an individual by forcing medication to alter those thoughts without the consent of the patient, or unless there is an emergency or the patient is incompetent to refuse the treatment offered.

Competency and Informed Consent

Not only are confidentiality, privilege, and privacy interrelated, but obviously so are the concepts of *informed consent* and *competency* involved in these deliberations. Informed consent is but one type of consent necessary in the treatment of individuals. Other types of consent (Rada, 1976) include *implied consent* (which is involved, for example, in taking routine blood specimens or X-rays), *presumed consent* (involved when giving life-saving treatment to an unconscious patient who presumably would give consent if awake) and *vicarious consent* (that given by a parent, guardian, or conservator when the patient is incapable of consenting).

Informed consent involves the giving of proper information by the treater or the mental health professional in order for the patient to give a proper consent to treatment. This concept originated in surgery and medicine where doctors were required to give particular information to patients before operating on them. Patients had the right to know what the doctor was going to do, what effect that would have in terms of morbidity or mortality probability, what side-effects or after-effects patients could expect, and what alternative forms of treatment were available. In mental health practice, the professional is expected to discuss with patients the types of treatment available for a particular illness, the side-effects of such treatment, what alternative treatments would be available, and what might happen to them if they did not receive any treatment. These issues are particularly important in somatic treatments in psychiatry. These include psychosurgery (which has been virtually eliminated from the treatment modalities at present), electroshock treatment, and use of psychotropic medication. The major focus in recent legislation has been on the use of medication, primarily because of its side-effects and the difficulties encountered in monitoring them.

The questions have always been: How much information is necessary? Can one give too much information and thereby deter the patient from taking the necessary treatment? There are no particular guidelines regarding how much information is necessary, but some have indicated that side-effects that are not serious should be reported if they have an incidence of 5 percent or greater. Major side-effects should be discussed with the patient if their incidence is 1 percent or greater. Certainly, every patient receiving psychotropic medication should be told of the possibility of dry mouth, difficulty urinating, constipation, possible skin rashes, and, of course, tardive dyskinesia. If one frightens a patient excessively by telling in great detail what could happen—even though it is not likely to happen—and the patient does not take the necessary treatment, the doctor may have legal difficulties. There have been instances where treaters have been sued for preventing a patient from taking life-saving or necessary treatment by being excessively detailed or frightening in their descriptions of the possibilities of such treatment. Thus, in the practice of psychotherapy or mental health treatment, it becomes an art to determine how much to tell the patient and what to withhold.

Nevertheless, the patient does require sufficient information on which to base a proper consent for treatment. This implies the patient is competent to make such a decision about the treatment. *Competency* is another issue that must be defined properly and placed into perspective in these deliberations. (See Chapter 9, on Civil Competency, for a more complete discussion.) Competency is not an all-encompassing matter, but is specific for particular questions within the law. Competency often refers to a person's ability to manage his own affairs; that is, whether or not the person is of such sound mind that he knows who he is, where he is, what the date is, and how much money he has and in what form, and that he is not subject to the will of designing persons intending fraudulently to deprive him of his money. But that is only one type of competency. Competency to write a will involves a person's understanding that she is writing a will, as well as her knowledge of the nature and extent of her bounty and the natural objects of her affection. That is, does she know approximately how much money she has and to whom she could leave her assets?

In order to be competent to testify in court (testimonial capacity), a person must know the nature of the court proceedings and his role within them. He also must be able properly to identify people and items that may be presented to him. Other forms of competency include competency to vote, to enter into a contract, to stand trial in criminal matters, or to get married or divorced. Generally, to be competent for any of these items, the person must know the nature and consequences of the situation in which he is involved. Thus, in order to be competent to enter into a contract, a person must know the nature of the proceedings of that contract and the consequences of his involvement.

In one particular case, I was asked by a woman to testify in court that she was a competent mother. I had treated the woman for five years and knew a great deal about her. If I am called to testify, I may be asked any question about the patient that is relevant to the issue of her proper care of her children. I may be asked about her consistency of care of the children, whether she has ever abandoned them or left them for long periods of time, whether she has been physically brutal to them, whether she has tried to kill herself, and other such questions. Since all of these matters had been part of her history and I had been privy to them through her communications to me, I was concerned about the advisability of my testifying. I believed that she had a right to know that the questions might be asked and to know how I would answer them. I felt it was especially important for her to have this information. After fully apprising her of the situation in which she was involved, she competently agreed to have me testify, despite the harm that could come to her if the information were revealed. Had I not given her the information beforehand, I would have felt I had not properly advised her about the waiver of her privilege she incurred by asking me to testify. She could have refused to allow me to testify had she known the nature and consequences of my testimony.

Thus, the mental health professional–patient relationship is considered to be one of trust, equal to that of any fiduciary relationship. The patient should feel confident that the communications he gives to his treater will not be divulged inappropriately but may be disclosed under proper legal compulsion or with his informed consent.

Of recent consideration are the Freedom of Information Act of 1972 and the Privacy Amendment of 1974. Although these laws pertain primarily to individuals seeking information about themselves which may affect their lives and their future, it has been determined that patients have the right to see their records if they choose to do so. This may be done under controlled situations and circumstances where harmful information can be processed properly with the patient to minimize the degree of harm. As much as patients have a right to keep their records from being improperly disclosed, they also have a right to the information contained in their records that may affect them and their future. This is true of all information about a patient, even that sent to insurance companies, third-party payers, courts, or other authorities requiring information. How much to disclose and under what circumstances is part of the art of caring for patients.

There are several means by which such disclosure may be made with the consent of the patient. In Pennsylvania, the Mental Health Act (1976) specifically prohibits releasing any "confidential" information without the informed consent of the patient, except under three or four circumstances, including releasing information to subsequent treaters, to the county administrator, and to courts under proper legal compulsion. The Mental Health Act, however, continues that "privileged" communications may not be disclosed to anyone, without exception, without the written informed consent of the patient. In these cases, the definition of *privileged communications* is that information given directly to the treater by the patient; whereas *confidential information* is that information obtained by the treater from sources other than the patient.

One may release information with the consent of the patient by either having the patient sign a consent form that is properly dated and time limited (probably not valid after three months), with the patient reading the information that is to be disclosed. One also may mail the information to the patient, who in turn may mail directly to the source of inquiry. Thus, the patient will take the responsibility for disclosing the information, both psychologically and practically. One may read the information to the patient over the telephone or mail her a copy of what is sent to the third-party payer or other source of inquiry.

In all respects, the conduct of the mental health professional toward the patient must demonstrate trust, respect, and dignity for the patient. To the extent possible, the patient should participate in decisions about her treatment and the consequences of information that is revealed about her. She is to be considered competent in these matters unless proven to be incompetent by a court of law. If she is proven incompetent and a guardian is appointed for her, then all matters of this type must be dealt with directly through the guardian. As we will see, the implications of the concepts of this chapter have far-reaching effects in other phases of the care and treatment of the mentally ill.

References

American Medical Association Statement of Ethics. *American Journal of Psychiatry, 130*:9, September 1973, 1061–1064.

American Psychiatric Association Statement of Ethics. Section 9. *American Journal of Psychiatry, 130*:9, September 1973, 1063–1064.

Freedom of Information Act. 5 USC Sect. 552, 1972.

In Re B: Appeal of Dr. Loren Roth. 150, March Term, Supreme Court of Pa., Western District, 1977.

McIntosh v. Milano. 168 NJ Super., 466 Law Div., 1979.

Pennsylvania Act 143. Pennsylvania Statutes, 1976.

Privacy Act. 5 USC Sect. 552(a), 1974.

Rada, R. T. Informed Consent in the Care of Psychiatric Patients. *National Association of Private Psychiatric Hospitals Journal, 8,* 1976, 9–12.

Tarasoff v. The Regents of the University of California et al. 529 P. 2d, 553 Ca., 1974.

Chapter 2

Keeping Records for Mentally Ill Patients

Record keeping on the mentally ill and emotionally disturbed has become increasingly regulated over the past two decades. The issue has been confusing to most practitioners, who are concerned about having excessive detail in the patient's records that may be subpoenaed or taken from their offices for use in matters over which they have little or no control. Others would like to have all the information in records in the event they are sued by their patients. They then would be able to document every detail and aspect of the treatment, for their own protection in the event of a lawsuit.

Both extremes appear to be possible but not very common. Some psychiatrists have advocated keeping only what is known as "IRS data" in order to satisfy the requirements of the Internal Revenue Service for record keeping on income and expenditures. They advocate no other information about the patient in the record except perhaps the kind of medication he was taking, any side-effects of the medication, perhaps a diagnosis, and, even less likely, a prognosis. This may be fine for outpatient private psychotherapy for some people, but it is not recommended for hospital record keeping or inpatient services. It is not recommended even for outpatient clinic cases where greater documentation of illness, progress, and behavior should be included. Perhaps the ideal lies somewhere between the two extremes of including great detail or including little or nothing.

Freedom of Information

Since the Freedom of Information Act of 1972, patients have a right to read their medical and psychiatric records. For medical purposes the records may not be terribly harmful to patients, but some psychiatric records contain information that could affect the patients adversely. In this case, it may not be in the patients' best interests to review these records, so some means of helping them with the information they receive from reading their records would be important. Some hospitals have developed a system whereby patients have access to records but only after completing a detailed application, and then only under specific guidelines. If the treating psychiatrist or the physician in charge of the clinic determines from reviewing a patient's records that information could affect her patient adversely, she may wish to sit with the patient and help interpret some of it. Some hospital staff have openly withheld particular parts of the record out of concern that the patient would have a negative reaction to its disclosure.

Disclosure of Information

Perhaps an even greater concern on the part of treaters is the disclosure of information to third parties. There are legitimate third parties who require information about patients, mostly the third-party payers such as Blue Cross, Blue Shield, Major Medical, and other insurance companies. Also, courts and administrative agencies may require information in the management of their cases.

Particular guidelines have been developed for disclosure of such information under specific circumstances. Blue Shield, Blue Cross, and Major Medical insurance companies have developed simplified forms that require basic information that does not go beyond data required for payment. It is important to note that there has to be a balance of revealing information and withholding it. Insurance companies must have justification for the spending of money, even though it is legitimate; thus, they do require basic data and information in order to complete transactions between themselves and medical services. An example of a violation of ethics in this area is the insurance company that sent an unduly long, detailed form asking the clinician to document transference and countertransference phenomena in the patient. This material is irrelevant; the form was returned unanswered to the insurance company, and copies were sent to the Underwriters Association, the Medical Society, and the Bar Association, suggesting that the insurance company be required to modify it to conform with the standards of other third-party payers. The important point here is that irrelevant information need not be sent, even though it is requested. The clinician should confine his responses to relevant data necessary to justify the medical expenditure. He also should obtain informed consent from his patient before sending any forms to an insurance company.

Often the form will be accompanied by a release-of-information consent form that the patient may have signed, possibly several years earlier. The clinician should honor release-of-information forms that are signed, current, properly dated, and time limited. She also should consult the patient, whenever possible, to confirm the patient's wishes to have the information disclosed. The patient may decide to refuse to disclose the information, even at the risk of having his medical payments denied.

Courts may require disclosure of information about people who are brought before them in various circumstances. (See Chapter 1, discussion of privileged communications, confidentiality, and waivers of privilege.) In one case in California (*In Re: Lifschutz*, 1970), a patient who had been injured in a fight had sued his assailant and family for damages resulting from the attack. He claimed, along with physical damages, that he had mental and emotional injuries and named Dr. Joseph Lifschutz as his previous therapist. Inasmuch as he had raised his mental state as an issue before the court and named Dr. Lifschutz as a prior psychotherapist, he had waived his privilege to Dr. Lifschutz' silence. Dr. Lifschutz, however, believed he had a voice in the matter and declined to produce his records after they had been subpoenaed. He then was issued a direct order by the court to produce his records; he refused, arguing that his psychoanalytic treatment with the patient was protected by rules of confidentiality and that he could invoke the privilege of the therapist–patient relationship. The judge denied his contention, indicating the privilege belonged to the patient, who had waived his privilege of Dr. Lifschutz' silence. Dr. Lifschutz then was held in contempt of court, and he appealed to the Court of Appeals of California. That court upheld the lower court's decision, so Dr. Lifschutz appealed to the Supreme Court of California, which upheld the lower court's decision as well. Dr. Lifschutz continued to refuse to reveal his records and was sent to prison as a penalty for contempt of court. After several days in prison, he was allowed to show his records to the judge *in camera*, that is, in the privacy of the judge's chambers. The judge evaluated their relevancy in this particular case and ruled the records were not relevant and that Dr. Lifschutz did not have to testify. That case reaffirmed the statute that states that the privilege belongs to the patient and not to the psychotherapist.

There is one exception to that general rule, however, which exists in Illinois. In that state, the privilege belongs to the therapist in domestic relations matters where the psychotherapist agrees to work with a couple having marital difficulties, in an effort to salvage the marriage. Under Illinois law, that psychotherapist is precluded from ever testifying for or against either party in any hearing relating to their domestic relations matters. In this way, the State of Illinois can guarantee absolute confidentiality, privacy, and secrecy to the members of a family wishing to obtain help without concern that what the family may say in therapy may be turned against them subsequently in a court of law. This action is necessary to encourage openness within the therapeutic situation.

The argument for privilege belonging to the patient and not to the therapist focuses directly on this issue. The patient cannot feel free to be as completely open and honest with his therapist if he has any concern that what he says in therapy may be divulged later in court against his wishes.

In private outpatient treatment, the disclosure of information always must be with informed consent of the patient. There are several means of achieving this goal:

1. The treater may dictate, in the presence of the patient, the report that is to be sent out.
2. The treater may mail the completed report to the patient for her to release to the third party requiring the information.
3. The treater may call the patient on the telephone, read to her what has been written, and obtain her consent to release the information directly to the third party.
4. The treater may call the patient on the telephone, receive her approval, and then mail her a copy of the information that is disclosed to another person. In order to release the information, the treater must have a release-of-information form that is dated, time limited, and signed by the patient.
5. The therapist may notify the patient at the beginning of treatment that it is understood that a particular insurance company or third party (e.g., probation officer) will receive regular reports, if that is part of the requirement for treatment. This should be understood by the patient, who gives his consent as part of the treatment. Each time a report is sent, the patient should be informed of the contents of the report.

Content of Records

Seeing that disclosure of records is regulated by law, the treater often wonders what should be placed in the record and what should be withheld. Lawyers say that everything that happens in therapy should be put in the record so that it may be reviewed later by a third party, in the event of a conflict or a lawsuit. Treaters, on the other hand, feel that sensitive material should not be included. Recently the feasibility of keeping dual sets of records—a primary and secondary set—has been discussed. In private practice, there is no legal justification at the present time for this; however, there is justification, in teaching institutions, for students, residents, and interns to keep in the records only that which is pertinent and relevant to the treatment of the patient. Other speculative psychodynamic configurations that enhance teaching within the field should be kept in a teaching notebook that belongs to the student, in order that she obtain full benefit of her learning experience.

These notes do not form a part of the record and should not be kept with the main chart. Psychoanalytic notes, taken by the psychoanalyst behind the couch, also should not be included in the record. These are memory joggers for the therapist's own use. It may be best for the psychoanalyst to summarize, or to put in very constricted form, the notes she wishes to have as part of the record on her patient. For the clinical psychologist in training, speculative psychodynamics obtained from use of psychological tests also should be used as teaching material and not as primary record material. Only the standard form of responses and raw data for the testing should be included in the record; or else the summary report should be in the record, with the raw data available if required or needed at a later date.

Records will contain different information, depending on the agency or source of treatment and the inclination of the treater. All records should contain the following basic data:

1. The patient's name and any aliases
2. The patient's address
3. The patient's telephone number if available
4. The patient's age
5. The patient's race
6. The patient's sex
7. Any unusual identifying information
8. The dates that the patient appeared in treatment or for evaluation, and the major concern of the patient; that is, the reason he is coming, or was sent, for treatment or evaluation.
9. The evaluation of the treater as to diagnosis or basic evaluation of the patient
10. A treatment plan, proposal, or recommendation
11. Whether or not the patient takes any medication for the condition for which he seeks treatment; any side-effects or unusual reactions to different kinds of medication
12. Previous medical history, including such details as previous hospitalizations, operations, fractures, head injuries, blackouts, medications taken, response to various medications, and illnesses
13. Possibly educational, family, marital, occupational, and social histories
14. Details of the patient's sex life, if pertinent or relevant to the evaluation; for example, if the person is being evaluated by a forensic psychiatrist for the charge of rape, a detailed sexual history would be necessary and essential in the record
15. A diagnosis of the patient, if available, and if the evaluator is so inclined; using *DSM-III* numbers and labels may or may not be

important, but for statistical and accountability purposes it may be relevant

16. A treatment plan and prognosis or estimated time of treatment, especially in cases involving third-party payments or lawsuits where insurance companies need to estimate how long the treatment will continue and how much it will cost

Material that is not essential to the record includes:

1. Third party statements about the patient
2. Hearsay information garnered from indirect sources, except if relevant
3. Arrest record, unless relevant
4. Detailed sexual history, unless relevant

It should be stated very clearly that the patient's records should be kept in a safe place that is not easily accessible to others. Preferably, they should be locked for protection. A recent case in California, which reached the Supreme Court of the United States (*Zurcher* v. *Stanford Daily Federal Register*, 1978), indicated that federal law-enforcement agencies pursuing criminal investigations may obtain search warrants to confiscate psychiatrists' records. The search warrants may be used in obtaining documentary evidence, such as medical records, from persons not suspected of having committed a crime but who may have information that would help in the law-enforcement investigation. Thus, all psychiatrists' or mental health professionals' records may be searched with the aid of a search warrant. The difference is that a hearing need not be held to show cause why the search should occur. The law-enforcement agents may come into the psychotherapist's office, on the basis of the search warrant alone, and obtain the records before such a hearing is held. At the time of this writing there have been no incidents of search and seizure of psychiatrists' files; however, the mental health professional is put on notice that this possibility exists and therefore should safeguard his records accordingly.

Records should be maintained in as legible a form as possible, with clear handwriting and the use of proper grammar and only common and recognized abbreviations. Alterations should not be made in records unless necessary. In the event an alteration is required, it should be handled as follows:

1. The record should never be erased.
2. A line should be drawn through the erroneous material in the chart and the corrected version substituted.
3. The correction should be dated and initialed.

4. A chart should never be altered after material has been subpoenaed in a lawsuit. This may be considered tampering with evidence and could result in a serious penalty.

In one case the hospital records had been obtained by a plaintiff's attorney prior to formal subpoena or court order. When the lawyer later obtained the official records by subpoena, he noted variations, erasures, and modifications from the original record he had obtained. Needless to say, the judge was quite disturbed at the intentional changing of records, done in order to protect the physician who initially had erred with his patient.

Records should be kept for at least five to seven years, for legal purposes. The statute of limitation, i.e., the length of time during which a legal action may be instituted for tort (noncriminal wrong) action or malpractice, is two years. This does not mean the statute runs out two years after the last time a patient was seen; rather, it runs out two years after the patient knew or should have known the damage was incurred as a result of treatment. That knowledge may not occur for some time after the final session of therapy. It is probably wise to keep records indefinitely, since patients may return for treatment even as long as 15 or 20 years after initial contact. It would be helpful to have the early information available for comparison when the patient subsequently returns for treatment.

The basic purpose of keeping records on patients is to provide the therapist with a means of communication about the patient. Perhaps the current therapist needs to refresh her recollection of the patient from time to time, or maybe a subsequent therapist requires information in order to treat the patient properly. Thus, the quality and content of the records are important.

Some patients may refuse to give permission to have their medical records sent to a subsequent treating facility. Involuntary patients do not have that option, however, since the court has ordered them to a particular hospital for treatment. The hospital personnel require the medical records in order to treat the patient appropriately. In fact, it has been found that therapists who do not request prior medical records fall below the standard of care in the event a lawsuit is instituted, because they failed to obtain adequate data for proper decision making about their patients.

On the other hand, voluntary patients may refuse to have their records sent to the next treating facility. Similarly, the new therapist may refuse to treat the patient unless the records are made available. It should not be taken for granted that because a patient volunteers for treatment that he automatically consents to have his records sent to the next doctor. He should be given every opportunity to make decisions about every phase of his treatment.

Subpoena of Records

In the event that a clinician receives a subpoena for her medical records, what steps may she take? First, she should contact the attorney who issues the subpoena to determine his reasons for obtaining the records, when he wants them, and whether it is appropriate that he have them. If there is any question that his purpose is not appropriate or legitimate, then it is proper to withhold the records until a court order is obtained or until a hearing may be held. In the event of a hearing, it is essential to be represented by counsel. The attorney for the hospital or the clinic, or one's own private attorney, should be consulted for advice before entering the courtroom.

If it is determined that the purpose for obtaining records is appropriate and legitimate and will not be harmful to the patient, it is still wise for the therapist to contact the patient to tell him that his records have been subpoenaed and to allow him the opportunity to resist if he chooses. Very often, however, it is the patient who wishes his records to be released, in order to institute a lawsuit.

It should be noted that the records belong to the person who prepares them, that is, the therapist or clinician who makes the record, or the hospital in which the patient has been treated. The hospital librarian is the custodian of the records that belong to the hospital. The therapist is the custodian of the records that she prepares. The information contained within the record belongs to the patient and is available to him if he wishes this information.

Summary

The keeping of records on mentally ill patients has become a highly regulated, complex issue. Clinicians and practitioners and all mental health professionals must be aware of the rules and regulations governing the preparation, maintenance, and disclosure of records on their patients. Patients' access to their records is governed by certain guidelines that aim at ensuring that patients will not be harmed by reading the information contained therein. If there is any question of harm to patients reading their records, then clinicians or mental health professionals must be available to help patients interpret or deal with the material.

References

In Re: Lifschutz. 85 Cal. Rep. 829, 476 P. 2d, 557 Cal. Superior Court, April 15, 1970.
Zurcher v. Stanford Daily Federal Register. 436 U.S., 547, April 17, 1978.

Chapter 3

Involuntary Hospitalization of the Mentally Ill

Historically, the mentally ill were considered to be violent, uncontrollable, irrational people who required not only hospitalization but also restraints and medication and various devices for helping the patients control their behavior. The decision was seen as a medical one, requiring psychiatrist or a physician to declare a person mentally ill and in need of hospitalization. At first, only one physician was required for commitment; later, this was changed to a two-physician requirement, to prevent any one doctor who was friendly with the family from acting in collusion with the family to hospitalize a person against his will. Shortly afterward, the law required a due process hearing by a judge, to hear the testimony of the psychiatrists who independently examined the person and declared him in need of hospitalization.

The Lessard Case

Perhaps the case most clearly ushering in the new era on involuntary commitment of the mentally ill was that of *Lessard* v. *Schmidt* (1972). In that case, Alberta Lessard was apprehended on October 29, 1971 and taken to a mental health center in Milwaukee. The police officers who picked her up filled out the emergency detention form and Ms. Lessard was admitted on an emergency basis. Two days later, the police officers testified before the judge, who ordered continuing confinement for the next ten days. A few days later, a psychiatrist filed an application with the judge, indicating that Ms. Lessard was suffering from schizophrenia and recommending permanent commitment, which was granted. Her commitment period was extended several times (usually from 30 to 60 days) until the two physicians appointed by the judge could examine her and report back to the court. The judge also appointed a guardian *ad litem* to represent her. In addition, Ms. Lessard retained counsel through the Milwaukee Legal Services. Her commitment period was increased and continued without notice and without a due-process hearing, except that the judge found Ms. Lessard to be "mentally ill." The commitment order was extended for another month, although Ms. Lessard was allowed to go home on outpatient "parole" basis.

In her complaint before the District Court, Ms. Lessard alleged that the procedure in Wisconsin for involuntary civil commitment denied her due process of law for the following reasons:

1. It permitted involuntary detention for a possible maximum period of 145 days without benefit of hearing.
2. It failed to make mandatory the notice of all hearings.
3. It failed to give adequate and timely notice where notice was given.
4. It failed to provide for mandatory notice of right to trial by jury.
5. It failed to give a right to counsel or appointment of counsel at a meaningful time.
6. It failed to permit counsel to be present at psychiatric interviews.
7. It failed to provide for exclusion of hearsay evidence and for the privilege against self-incrimination.
8. It failed to provide access to an independent psychiatric examination by a physician of her choice.
9. It permitted commitment of a person without determination beyond a reasonable doubt that the person was in need of commitment.
10. It failed to describe the standard for commitment.

The court found that the Wisconsin civil commitment procedure was constitutionally defective in so far as it

1. Failed to require effective and timely notice of the "charges" under which a person was detained
2. Failed to require adequate notice of all rights, including the right to jury trial
3. Permitted detention longer than needed.

The court ordered changes in the proceedings in Wisconsin and ordered the defendants, that is, the State of Wisconsin, to submit a memorandum at the end of a 90-day period detailing the procedures taken to dispose of the cases involved and describing their efforts to implement the order, especially to provide for proper outpatient treatment.

This decision by the District Court was appealed to the Supreme Court of the United States, where the judgment was vacated and the case remanded to the District Court. Later, in 1974, the District Court set out more specifically what it had said in the earlier decision. Wisconsin again appealed to the United States Supreme Court, where in May 1975 the District Court's opinion again was vacated and remanded. Nevertheless, Lessard v. Schmidt was the first case to state specifically the procedural safeguards for involuntary commitment of the mentally ill. Most commitment statues that have been written since 1975 include the procedural safeguards outlined in the Lessard case.

Dangerousness

A second major change in commitment proceedings involves the concept of dangerousness. Formerly, a person could be committed to the state hospital involuntarily if he were shown to be mentally ill and in need of hospitalization. However, mental health attorneys began arguing the merits of the thesis of John Stuart Mill in his work, *On Liberty* (1859):

> The only purpose for which power can be rightfully exercised over any member of a civilized community, against his will, is to prevent harm to others. His own good, either physical or moral, is not a sufficient warrant. He cannot rightfully be compelled to do or forebear because it will be better for him to do so, because it will make him happier, because, in the opinions of others, to do so would be wise, or even right. [p. 22]

Thus, hospitalizing a person for his own good under the *parens patria* doctrine of the state is not sufficient to detain a person against his will. A person must be shown to be dangerous to others in order to detain him for treatment.

The United States Supreme Court, in the case of *O'Connor v. Donaldson* (1975), said there can be no trade-off for involuntarily hospitalizing a person merely for the sake of treatment. The *quid pro quo* theory, that is, hospitalization for treatment, or deprivation of liberty in order to provide treatment, will not fly. One of the reasons given by the Supreme Court was that treatment is not precise and the definition and diagnosis of mental illness is even less precise; so it would not be fair to lock a person up against his will in order to provide an uncertain treatment for a poorly defined illness.

However, the police power of the state may come into play in involuntary commitment proceedings. The state has the obligation to protect its citizens; it can protect a person from himself, and must protect the safety of others from the violence of the mentally ill person by commitment for treatment.

The standards of commitment, then, must include in some form the concept of dangerousness. The problem is in the definition of that concept. Dangerousness has not been defined clearly in any jurisdiction, and attempts made to define it have been relatively unsuccessful. Kozol and others (1972), for example, define dangerousness as "a potential for inflicting serious bodily harm on another" (p. 371). With that definition, most people could be considered dangerous under certain clinical conditions. Goldzband (1973) considers dangerousness to be "the quality of an individual or a situation leading to the potential or actuation of harm to an individual, community or a social order" (p. 371). This definition provides a sociological attempt at grappling with dangerousness. Heller (1968) gives us a complex psychodynamically oriented definition when he states

> . . . dangerousness then may be viewed as either a transient or a lasting state of impairment of certain ego functions . . . secondary to a variety of constitutional, organic, psychologic, developmental or environmental factors, and resulting in a recognizable deterioration of the specific functions of judgment, self observation and the capacity to defend against anxiety or tension. [pp. 26–27]

These three definitions are all different and all lacking in some regard the precision that is needed to apply such a definition to commitment proceedings. Perhaps the definition in the Mental Health Act of Pennsylvania (Pennsylvania Act 143, 1976) is more appropriate; certainly it is much better for application to the mentally ill. That definition indicates that a person, to be committed as an emergency involuntary patient, must be examined by a physician and the commitment proceed within 30 days of the examination. The person to be committed must have been found to be suffering from a serious mental illness or disorder such that she has exhibited behavior or threat of behavior within the past 30 days that would lead to harm to others or to herself. The three major types of harm are suicide, physical destruction, and neglect that leads to physical destruction. There also must be the prediction that without hospitalization the behavior would continue within the next 30 days so the patient's safety or the safety of others would be in jeopardy. Here, predictions are being made on the basis of past performance under certain clinical conditions that can be assessed by the mental health professional.

What is less clear and more difficult to accept is the testimony that a person is both mentally ill and dangerous, made by the mental health professional without the clinical guidelines necessary to making a prediction of future violent behavior. It is not sufficient to testify that a person is dangerous without describing what clinical entities are involved and what guidelines have been used in formulating both the opinion and the prediction.

The use of dangerousness as a criterion for involuntary hospitalization has its merits, as indicated in the police power of the state to protect its citizens, but it also has its drawbacks. These lie not only in the difficulty of defining it but also in the implications of its application as a criterion for involuntary commitment. These drawbacks include danger to the patient, danger to those treating the patient, and danger to the community.

Danger to the Patient

Steadman & Cocozza (1974) have demonstrated in their research that psychiatrists cannot predict accurately the dangerousness of a mentally ill patient. If one accepts their conclusions, then the patient will be in danger if the psychiatrist has the responsibility for making such predictions that affect the patient's liberty. If the psychiatrist is overly cautious and overpredicts dangerousness, the patient may remain in the hospital excessively long and be deprived of his liberty or his right to the least restrictive alternative of treatment. If, however, the psychiatrist underpredicts dangerousness, the patient may be released prematurely to the community and may be unable to handle the stress of his new environment. He may break down in the community and express violence to himself or to others. Alternatively, he may be victimized or exploited by others in the community because of his inability to handle the stress of the community.

A case in point is *State* v. *Davee* (1977), in which the Supreme Court of Missouri upheld the decision of a lower-court judge not to release Mr. Davee to the community, even though psychiatrists had testified that he was no longer mentally ill and no longer could benefit from the traditional treatment the hospital had to offer. The Supreme Court, considering Mr. Davee to be dangerous (though presumably not mentally ill, according to the psychiatrists), redefined treatment in the hospital to include "observation and containment," in order to justify Mr. Davee's retention. Since that case was decided in 1977, newer legislation has overturned the effect of that decision; however, one can note the danger to the patient of remaining in a hospital when he is no longer mentally ill but merely "dangerous."

Danger to the Psychiatrist and Other Treaters

Psychiatrists have held themselves up as experts in predicting dangerousness when they have testified at commitment hearings. They also have indicated such an expertise when they have made assessments for people on parole or probation. Thus, it is not surprising that courts have held the mental health professional as an expert in making such predictions despite the studies of Steadman & Cocozza (1974) and others. It follows logically that if the psychiatrist is an expert in the prediction of dangerousness, he also must be an expert in the prediction of nondangerousness; that is to say, he must be able to predict when his patient, who has been hospitalized as both mentally ill and dangerous, becomes no longer mentally ill and no longer dangerous and therefore ready for discharge.

The danger to the mental health professional in making such a prediction lies in his vulnerability to lawsuit if his prediction is inaccurate and the patient becomes violent either to himself or to others. Recently, a number of lawsuits have emerged charging the clinician with the legal responsibility for the patient's violent behavior. The argument is that the psychiatrist prematurely discharged the patient when he knew, or should have known, that the patient was dangerous.

A second danger to the mental health professional in predicting dangerousness has emerged in the case of *Tarasoff* v. *The Regents of the University of California* (1974), in which the therapist has been held to have a special relationship with a third-party victim of the violence of her patient. That is, if a patient tells his psychotherapist that he is going to kill or harm a third person, the therapist is expected to breach the confidentiality of her therapist–patient relationship and protect or warn the intended victim of the patient's violence. The Supreme Court of California has indicated that the therapist has a special duty to that third party and may be held liable if she does not communicate her patient's threats of harm, provided she believes them. The Supreme Court also indicated that, if the violence occurs, there may be a presumption that the therapist should have known that her patient would be violent.

Danger to the Community

It goes without saying that if the patient is discharged prematurely—that is, before he is ready to go or when he is still "dangerous"—that the community may suffer from his violence. It is essential, under the newer mental health regulations providing for the least restrictive alternative of treatment, that the communities develop and implement proper community services for patients who are released to the community. Without such follow-up services, it becomes increasingly difficult to discharge patients to inadequate community facilities. Judges may make the decision with the help of the psychiatrist that patients should be retained in the hospital for treatment if there are no adequate facilities in the community. This may become a problem for the patient, but the judge must weigh the rights of the patient against his duty to protect the community.

Conclusions about Dangerousness

The American Psychiatric Association (1974) has stated clearly:

> It has been noted that "dangerousness" is neither a psychiatric nor a medical diagnosis but involves issues of legal judgment and definition, as well as issues of social policy. Psychiatric expertise in the prediction of "dangerousness" is not established and clinicians should avoid "conclusory" judgments in this regard. [p. 33]

Thus, the prediction of dangerousness is not a psychiatric matter alone. It is a social, judicial, legal, medical, and psychological decision that ought to be addressed in a comprehensive manner by a combination of disciplines. Prediction should not be left to therapists alone, for it has been shown that they do not have special expertise in this regard. They may offer the clinical approach, but there are other factors that must be considered. Decisions about dangerousness must be made by the judge, who is the representative of society in this regard. Decisions about discharge from the hospital, when a person is no longer dangerous, also should be made by a judge with proper input from multiple sources.

Persons who are dangerous but are not mentally ill should not be committed to hospitals nor retained in hospitals, since hospitals are meant to treat the mentally ill and not the dangerous. If mentally ill people who have been dangerous are considered for discharge, a monitoring system similar to probation should be developed to observe and treat them in the community as a condition of their release.

It has been shown clearly by many that violent people in our community are not necessarily mentally ill and, conversely, that the mentally ill are not necessarily violent. Although in some cases the two are connected, we must not equate mental illness with dangerousness or violence. The treatment of the violent person may be nonmedical, and alternative forms of disposition should be considered.

In sum, clinicians can add a particular dimension to the total assessment of dangerousness and violence; however, theirs is not the only—nor even the most important—assessment, and it should be combined with other resources for a comprehensive evaluation of the patient and community management.

Peszke (1975) and others have argued against the utilization of dangerousness as a criterion for hospitalization on the grounds that psychiatrists cannot predict dangerousness accurately. He also is concerned that the decision about hospitalization has been taken away from the physician and given to the judge. He would favor medical determination of treatment, rather than judicial.

Following an extensive review of the cases involved and the difficulties for mental health professionals, it appears that the decision is more than a clinical one, since deprivation of liberty is involved. I am in favor of the judge making the decision for involuntary hospitalization as long as she also will make the decision for release of the patient from confinement when the patient is no longer mentally ill. The difficulty in that recommendation lies in the possible occurrence of cases similar to *State* v. *Davee*, discussed previously. For a complete review and analysis of the problem of predicting dangerousness, see the excellent monograph by Monahan (1981).

Parens Patria Considerations

As long as dangerousness remains a criterion for involuntary hospitalization and deprivation of liberty, it should not be the exclusive reason for commitment; rather it should be one alternative, the other being the *parens patria* approach in which the patient is hospitalized because he is mentally ill and in need of hospital treatment. *Parens patria* is a viable consideration for commitment, as long as due process procedures and safeguards remain in effect.

Commitments following the procedures outlined in *Lessard* v. *Schmidt* (1972) and other cases have been seen to be antifamily. Judge Caesar (1980) has written a very interesting article entitled "Preserving the Family: A Brief for Limited Commitment of Non-Dangerous Mentally Ill Persons," in which he argues for retention of the *parens patria* approach in some cases, again, provided due process guidelines are upheld. I would strongly agree with the judge's concern that the utilization of dangerousness as a criterion for involuntary hositalization may exclude the previously effective *parens patria* approach. There is room for both in our extremely complex system. The concept of dangerousness, which is so poorly defined, should not be the exclusive factor in determining whether a person should be hospitalized against his will.

An argument has arisen as to the standard of proof needed for involuntary commitment. Patients and their representatives have argued that the standards should be a criminal standard of "beyond a reasonable doubt," since a person's liberty is at stake. Physicians and others giving testimony have argued for a more liberal standard of "preponderance of the evidence," as seen in civil cases. The United States Supreme Court in the case of *Addington* v. *Texas* (1979), proposed a moderate approach or middle ground standard of proof, that is, "clear and convincing evidence." Here they cited the need for a standard beyond the simple "preponderance of the evidence," or just over 50 percent certainty, but denied the claim for the "beyond a reasonable doubt" standard, which approaches 90 to 95 percent certainty. They said the person's liberty was at stake so the standard of proof should be higher than simple majority, but, since this is not a criminal matter and the person is not being confined for punishment but rather for treatment, the standard need not be 90 percent or beyond a reasonable doubt. The judges also alluded to the difficulty that clinicians have in making such predictions of dangerousness and need for confinement, thereby neutralizing the higher degree of proof.

Summary

The major changes in commitment of the mentally ill are the following. First, the criteria for involuntary hospitalization include the presence of mental illness that renders a person dangerous to himself or to others. *Parens patria* alone in most jurisdictions is not sufficient for hospitalization, but rather the concern of harm to self or others. Second, the procedures for commitment have changed. They now involve due process of law to protect the rights of the person at every step of the proceeding. He is entitled to have a lawyer present, to receive notice of a hearing, and to appeal his case to a higher court. The mentally ill person is no longer disenfranchised. He has working for him those mental health advocates who will uphold his rights, especially his right to liberty. He may be confined involuntarily only if his being at liberty jeopardizes the freedom and safety of others or of himself.

References

Addington v. Texas. 441 U.S. 418, 1979.

American Psychiatric Association. *Task Force Report 8, Clinical Aspects of the Violent Individual*. Washington, D.C.: American Psychiatric Association, July 1974, p. 33.

Caesar, B. Preserving the Family: A Brief for Limited Commitment of Non-Dangerous Mentally Ill Persons. *Journal of Marital and Family Therapy*, July 1980, 309–317.

Goldzband, M. G. Dangerousness. *Bulletin of the American Academy of Psychiatry and the Law, 1*, December 1973, 238–244.

Heller, M. S. Dangerousness, Diagnosis and Disposition. Proceedings of the Fourth Judicial Sentencing Institute, Crime Commission of Philadelphia, June 1968.

Kozol, H. L., Boucher, R. J., & Garofalo, R. F. The Diagnosis and Treatment of Dangerousness, *Crime and Deliquency*, 18, 1972, 371–392.

Lessard v. Schmidt. 49 Fed. Supp. 1078, U.S. District Court, Wisconsin, 1972.

Mill, J. S. *On Liberty*. 2d ed. London: Parker, 1859. As cited by Monahan, J. John Stuart Mill on the Liberty of the Mentally Ill: A Historical Note. *American Journal of Psychiatry, 134*, December 1977, 1428.

Monahan, J. The Clinical Prediction of Violent Behavior. Rockville, Md.: NIMH Publications, 1981.

O'Connor v. Donaldson. 422 U.S. 563, 1975.

Pennsylvania Act 143, Mental Health Act, 1976.

Peszke, M. A. *Involuntary Treatment of the Mentally Ill: The Problem of Autonomy*. Springfield, Ill.: Charles C Thomas, 1975.

State v. Davee. 558 S.W. 2d, 335 Mo., 1977.

Steadman, H., & Cocozza, J. *Careers of the Criminally Insane: Excessive Social Control of Deviants*. Lexington, Mass.: Lexington Books, 1974.

Tarasoff v. The Regents of the University of California et al. 529 P. 2d 553 Calif., 1974.

Chap

Patients' Rights to Treatment

The concept of the right to treatment was first enunciated by Morton Birnbaum in the *American Bar Association Journal* in 1960. Dr. Birnbaum, a lawyer and physician, espoused the notion of the right to adequate care and treatment of involuntarily committed mentally ill persons. He stated simply,

> It is proposed in this article that the courts under their traditional powers to protect the constitutional rights of our citizens begin to consider the problem of whether or not a person who has been institutionalized solely because he is sufficiently mentally ill to require institutionalization for care and treatment actually does receive adequate medical treatment so that he may regain his health, and therefore his liberty, as soon as possible; that the courts do this by means of recognizing and enforcing the right to treatment; and, that the courts do this, independent of any action by any legislature, as a necessary and overdue development of our present concept of due process of law. [Birnbaum, 1960, p. 504]

The Rouse Case

It was not until six years later that the first major case, *Rouse* v. *Cameron* (1966) in Washington, D.C. supported Birnbaum's concept. In that case Rouse was charged with a criminal act, was found not guilty by reason of insanity, and was sent to St. Elizabeth's Hospital for treatment. He claimed, however, that he did not receive treatment while in the hospital and in effect was confined against his will, essentially as a prisoner. Judge David Bazelon decided that, in this case, holding Mr. Rouse without treatment was tantamount to incarceration or preventive detention for no wrong doing and ordered Rouse to be released. Judge Bazelon set no standards or guidelines but did establish a statutory precedent for psychiatric patients' rights to treatment.

The Wyatt Case

Several years later, one of the most significant right-to-treatment cases emerged as a class-action suit in Alabama (*Wyatt* v. *Stickney*, 1972). The lawyers who brought this suit did so with great calculation, finding the right judge in the right state to pursue their claim that patients who were confined against their will were not receiving adequate treatment. The class-action suit was brought, in the name of Ricky Wyatt, in hopes of establishing the duty of the State of Alabama to provide proper care for all persons who were confined against their will to the hospitals in Alabama. Thus, the purpose of the lawsuit was to raise the quality of care for psychiatric patients and to prevent abuse of the mentally ill and the mentally retarded within the hospitals. Judge Frank Johnson heard the case and then asked the representative national organizations to provide him with guidelines or standards for adequate treatment. He was met with much opposition by organized medicine and psychiatry and by others who feared he would tell psychiatrists how to practice medicine. Psychiatrists saw this as an intrusion into their area of expertise and into their professional capacity. Judge Johnson did not specifically tell psychiatrists how to practice medicine; rather, he set general guidelines for adequate facilities and care of the mentally ill who were involuntarily confined. For example, he proclaimed the following patients' rights:

1. Freedom from unnecessary or excessive medication
2. Entitlement to weekly review by a physician of each patient's drug regimen, with prescriptions to terminate within 30 days
3. Requirement that treaters use the least restrictive conditions necessary to achieve the purposes of commitment
4. Freedom from treaters' use of medication as punishment or "substitute for program"
5. Freedom from physical restraint and isolation, except for emergencies
6. Freedom from experimental research without consent of the patient or next-of-kin, after review by Human Rights Committee
7. Freedom from submission to hazardous treatment without the patient's express and informed consent
8. Freedom from performing labor that interferes with treatment

He also ordered various temperatures, space requirements, and staff–patient ratios within the hospital. Many of these standards are in practice today. There was some initial criticism, both that the standards were too low and that they were too high, and that they could not be met with the finances available to the hospital system. There have been several cases similar to Wyatt's since 1971 that have continued the monitoring and implementation of Judge Johnson's original order.

The Donaldson Case

Another significant case in the area of the right to treatment is that of *Donaldson* v. *O'Connor* (1974). This case involved Kenneth Donaldson, a man who had spent 15 years at the Florida State Hospital at Chattahoochee, following his commitment by his parents for mental illness. Mr. Donaldson was not seen to be violent or in need of medication at any time during his hospital stay. He was kept in the hospital because the state law apparently allowed the doctors to keep him for treatment even though he was not dangerous. Mr. Donaldson sued the hospital for keeping him excessively long and without providing proper treatment. He also asked for punitive damages because he claimed the doctors kept him from outpatient treatment or less restrictive alternatives that were offered by various groups in other parts of the country. He was awarded $28,500 compensatory damages and $10,000 punitive damages by the Federal District Court. This was upheld by the Fifth Circuit Court of Appeals. In 1975, the United States Supreme Court declared that the case of *O'Connor* v. *Donaldson* (1975) was not a case of right to treatment, but rather a case involving right to liberty. The Supreme Court deferred deciding whether or not patients have a right to treatment but they did state the following:

> The finding of "mental illness" alone cannot justify a state's locking a person up against his will and keeping him indefinitely in simple custodial confinement. . . . In short a state cannot constitutionally confine without more a non-dangerous individual who is capable of surviving safely in freedom by himself or with the help of willing and responsible family members or friends.

Thus, the Supreme Court did not state whether there is a constitutional right to treatment; however, The Fifth Circuit Court of Appeals did so state, and Judge Bazelon declared there was a statutory right to treatment in the Washington, D.C. area.

Evolution of Patient's Bill of Rights

Organized medicine agreed that there is a constitutional right to treatment, and the American Psychiatric Association created a task force on the right to treatment, which issued a statement in 1977 (American Psychiatric Associa-

ıgnizing this right and the need for implementation and
it. The task force defined treatment "to include active in-
ı psychological, biological, physical, chemical, educational or
where application of the individual treatment plan is felt to have
expectation of improving the patient's condition" (p. 354).

This particular right is seen as the patient's right to receive treatment if he is to be locked up in a hospital for the purposes of treatment. Treatment does not mean medication alone, but it means the comprehensive approach as indicated in the task force statement and in Judge Johnson's guidelines and standards in the Wyatt case. For the first time, judges have begun to dictate the environment and criteria for the psychiatric treatment that they may expect mentally ill people to receive when they place them in the hospital against their will. The concern is that the patient has been deprived of his liberty and thus must be afforded compensatory rights.

Despite the fact that the Supreme Court did not recognize officially the involuntarily committed psychiatric patient's right to treatment, the need to provide adequate treatment for these patients has become generally recognized. In some hospitals, the Patient's Bill of Rights has been established, printed, and placed on the bulletin board where all may see it. Of course, it includes more than just patients' rights to treatment. Louis Kopolow, M.D., of the National Institute of Mental Health, Director of Patient Advocacy Programs, has listed a sample patient's bill of rights to include the following:

1. The right to be treated with dignity and respect by service providers and to have one's humanity recognized throughout the course of treatment
2. Freedom from unnecessary hospitalization
3. Freedom from unnecessary treatment
4. The right to information about one's treatment, including treatment philosophy, style, duration, cost, and likely outcome
5. The right to confidentiality
6. The right to high quality and effective services
7. The right to have services available when and where needed
8. The right to actively participate in treatment decisions and the establishment of priorities
9. The right to redress for grievances
10. The right to assistance of a patient advocate [Kopolow, 1976, pp. 201–202]

Thus, we can see that the right to adequate treatment and services is but one of many established rights of the mentally ill. Dr. Kopolow has written extensively on advocacy programs for patients and believes that, in order to promote and guarantee patients' rights, there has to be cooperation among these five major institutions and individuals:

1. The provider of services
2. Executive and legislative branches of the government
3. The judiciary
4. Insurance companies
5. The consumer

He suggests that psychiatrists and mental health professionals act as the advocates for patients' rights, since he believes that when patients' rights are in place and implemented, the patients' opportunities for improvement and successful response to treatment are enhanced.

Outpatients' Rights in the Community

Having established the concept of the right to adequate treatment within hospital settings, the next step for establishing patients' rights to treatment is in the communities after the patients have left the hospital. Priscilla Allen, a member of the President's Commission on the Treatment of the Mentally Disabled and herself a former patient, documents a bill of rights for outpatients that includes the following:

1. The right to voluntary treatment and/or services
2. The right to refuse treatment and/or services
3. The right to confidentiality of personal records
4. The right to utilize fully all economic rights and benefits
5. The right to maximum freedom, mobility and independence
6. The right to a humane psychological and physical environment
7. The right to information [Allen, 1976, p. 174]

Allen emphasizes that these rights for outpatients usually have been afforded to all citizens, but implies that there is a need for this bill of rights because, although these rights do in fact exist, they are not being implemented for the mentally ill in the communities.

One outstanding case in point supports Allen's contention: *Dixon* v. *Weinberger* (1975) in Washington, D.C. This case mandated effective outpatient services in the least restrictive alternative facility for those patients emerging from mental hospitals. It was found that inadequate facilities existed in the Washington, D.C. area; the court ordered the community to establish and provide competent services for patients who were sent for outpatient treatment and for those who had been discharged from the hospitals. Follow-up monitoring of the case has revealed that the system still fails to provide the required services. The immediate challenge in mental health is the provision of adequate services in the community for those patients who are not committable and for those who have been discharged recently from the hospitals.

Implications

Patients' rights considerations have placed the provider of services, or the mental health professional, in a difficult position. The professional is encouraged to give the least restrictive services available that are adequate and at the same time can protect both the patient and society, if and when necessary. Mental health professionals also may be placed in a difficult position because of the enactment of new legislation upholding the right to treatment, as well as the newer concepts of involuntary hospitalization based on police power and prediction of dangerousness. The clinician no longer can hospitalize the patient merely at the request of the family or if the patient is seen to be mentally ill without presenting a danger to himself or others. Family pressures on mental health professionals will increase as society encourages families to take more responsibility for their mentally ill members. We will need to develop newer facilities and outpatient services to provide least restrictive alternatives for those requiring treatment but who do not qualify for inpatient services. These changes present a major challenge to the mental health professional of all types in her care and treatment of the mentally ill. It will be important for psychiatrists, psychologists, psychiatric nurses, social workers, and other mental health professionals to learn to work effectively with other agencies of government and with the consumer in protecting and implementing patients' rights while continuing to be alert to relatively rapid changes in law affecting the care and treatment of mentally ill patients.

References

Allen, P. A Bill of Rights for Citizens Using Outpatient Mental Health Services. In H. R. Lamb (Ed.), *Community Survival for Long Term Patients*. San Francisco: Jossey Bass, 1976.

American Psychiatric Association. Task Force Report on the Right to Adequate Care and Treatment for the Mentally Ill and Mentally Retarded. *American Journal of Psychiatry*, 134:3, March 1977, pp. 354–355.

Birnbaum, M. The Right to Treatment. *American Bar Association Journal*, May 1960, p. 499–505.

Dixon v. Weinberger. 405 F. Supp. 974, D.D.C., 1975.

Donaldson v. O'Connor. 493 F. 2d 507, 5th Cir., 1974.

Kopolow, L. Patients' Rights and the Psychiatrists' Dilemma. *Bulletin of the American Academy of Psychiatry and the Law*, 4:3, 1976, 197–203.

O'Connor v. Donaldson. 422 U.S. 563, 1975.

Rouse v. Cameron, 373 F. 2d, 451 (D.C. scir. 1966).

Wyatt v. Stickney, 325 F. Supp. 381, M.D. Ala., 1972.

Chapter 5

Patients' Rights to Refuse Treatment

Emergence of the Right to Refuse Treatment

Perhaps one of the most confusing and difficult aspects of mental health law is the recently emerging right to refuse treatment. From a purely legal point of view, the patient has the right to refuse medication or other forms of treatment if he is involuntarily committed, is competent to make the decision about his treatment, and is not imminently violent to himself or others. Though this right has been declared as such, the issue actually emerges as one reflecting quality of care just as it does in right-to-treatment cases.

Relevant Court Cases

The emergence has been gradual and occasionally confused. One of the first cases is that of *Price* v. *Sheppard* (1976) in which electroshock therapy was declared as an "instrusive treatment" and therefore not allowed by the court against the patient's will if she were competent to decide against it's use. On the basis of that precedent, two subsequent cases in Minnesota were heard within a month of each other in contiguous counties. In one case (*In Re: Lundquist*, 1976) the court held that the injection of Prolixin was intrusive and therefore the patient legitimately could refuse it. In the other case (*In Re: Fussa*, 1976) the injection of Prolixin was not seen as intrusive and therefore the patient did not have the right to refuse it as treatment. Other right-to-refuse cases include *Winters* v. *Miller* (1971), which found that a person who has a religious repugnance to medication may not be forced to take medication unless that person's life is at stake or unless there is an emergency.

Perhaps the two most famous cases of right to refuse treatment include the Boston State Hospital case of *Rogers* v. *Okin* (1979) and the New Jersey class-action case of *Rennie* v. *Klein* (1979). In the Rogers case, Judge Tauro proclaimed that all patients who are involuntarily confined to the state hospitals have a right to refuse medication if they are competent and if they are not in an emergency state. He defined "emergency" as a situation in which a person is imminently violent to herself or others, and he mandated that a patient who is deemed to be incompetent must be so declared by a court of law.

In the Rennie case, Judge Brotman similarly held that patients have a right to refuse treatment unless they are incompetent to make the decision about their treatment or unless they pose a danger of emergency to the hospital. He defined "emergency" as a significant or sudden change in a patient's clinical status that would render him potentially harmful to himself or others. This is a different definition of emergency from that of Judge Tauro in the Rogers case and provides more flexibility in interpretation to the treating psychiatrist. Also, Judge Brotman, in the Rennie case, proclaimed that the patient may be functionally incompetent as deemed by the psychiatrist in charge rather than by a judicial opinion. Furthermore, Judge Brotman stated that treatment is a medical decision and whether or not a patient has the right to refuse may be determined better by an uninvolved psychiatrist appointed by the court.

Thus, one can see that the two cases are similar but easily distinguished one from the other. Judge Brotman heard several days of testimony in the first part of his decision and several more days in what is known as *Rennie* v. *Klein* (1979). He was concerned about the quality of care and the lack of implementation of his original order. Testimony was given that medication is used to control patients exclusively and is also the "end-all and be-all" of treatment. Monitoring of medication to prevent hazardous side-effects also was not done as competently as Judge Brotman would have expected within this hospital system. Thus, his order, couched in the form of a right, is in fact a comment on the quality of care within the state hospital system in New Jersey.

It seems clear that if patients were given adequate treatment and were not forced to take medication against their will, or were monitored properly where no damage resulted, that neither of these cases would have been brought. It seems clear also that if the mental health professionals had been able to provide a high quality of treatment within the hospital, the need for the right to treatment and right to refuse treatment lawsuits may either have been delayed or not have been brought at all.

The APA Viewpoint

Another way of looking at this situation is reflected by the American Psychiatric Association Task Force on the Right to Care and Treatment of the Mentally Ill and Mentally Retarded. In their statement, issued in 1977, they said the following:

> The American Psychiatric Association is aware of the possibility that the right to
> adequate care and treatment may be misunderstood and even be used in some

cases in a coercive manner. We therefore wish to clearly indicate that our concern is that adequate care and treatment be available. As is the practice generally in medicine, the patient's informed consent for treatment is required except for emergency situations.

No patient should be treated against his will unless some procedural safeguards are instituted. Since a patient's refusal of necessary treatment may not be in his best interest, some means of allowing him to receive proper medical care with the fewest time-consuming procedures must be developed. Depending on the circumstances, any of the following may be appropriate:

1. Court authorized treatment at the time of commitment
2. Court evaluation for competency to consent to or refuse treatment
3. In-hospital review committees (with outside representatives)
4. Administrative judicial hearings
5. Authorization for treatment on the basis of valid (legal) commitment certificates [American Psychiatric Association, 1977]

Thus, the controversy continues, and both the Rennie and Rogers cases have been appealed. The respective circuit courts of appeals have heard the cases and have modified them both. Rogers has been appealed to the United States Supreme Court, which has granted cert (agreed to hear arguments) and in the future undoubtedly will clarify the right-to-refuse issue.

Clinicians' Viewpoints

For many clinicians the right to refuse treatment appears to be "one right too many," as espoused by Steve Rachlin (1975). He has argued that, if a patient has the right to adequate treatment, he cannot also have the right to refuse that treatment. To him, that has seemed illogical. He has followed his original paper with a subsequent presentation (Rachlin, 1979) arguing that, if we believe in the *parens patria* approach (that is, that we hospitalize a person because he is ill and unable to take care of himself, not necessarily because he is dangerous to others or even imminently suicidal), that we cannot then logically accept the patient's right to refuse treatment. There would be no reason to put him in the hospital if we did not provide treatment.

The argument for this is that treatment is generally considered to mean a comprehensive treatment program including milieu therapy, psychotherapy, medication, nursing care, and other forms of treatment. No one appears to be arguing against any of the other forms of treatment except medication, primarily because of the potential dangers to patients from the effects of medication, especially if the patients are not properly observed, monitored, and treated. It is this particular concern that seems to be at issue at the present time. Thus, providing proper treatment with medication should result in providing patients both with their right to adequate treatment and their right

to refuse medication if they are competent and if they are not
violent. The right to refuse in such cases may be viewed as an inte,
the patient's right to adequate care and treatment. Certainly, the
medication has led in some cases to a more precise manner of tr
including one-on-one psychotherapy, segregation, soft restraints, aᴛᴜ other
specific forms of nonchemical therapy that help a patient deal with his
concerns and his fears. Ultimately, many patients may need medication after
other forms of treatment for acute crises are tried and fail to work adequately,
but at least, the other forms will have been tried we will have avoided the use
of medication when it was not absolutely necessary.

From a clinical point of view, the following fact is clear: There are certain
types of mental illnesses for which there is little or no treatment. Throughout
the ages, physicians have tried different forms of treatment, including blood
letting, tranquilizing chairs, hot and cold baths, electroshock therapy, insulin
coma, sleep therapy, and various types of drugs such as barbiturates and
narcotics. Since the mid 1950s and the advent of the psychotropic medications
for treatment of schizophrenia, psychiatrists have felt that there has been a
breakthrough in the treatment of the seriously mentally ill. Indeed, a number
of severely ill psychotics and schizophrenics have responded favorably to the
psychotropic medications, and many have been able to take treatment outside
of the hospital as a result of these rather specific drugs. It is important
therapeutically that psychiatrists feel they are doing something constructive
and positive for their patients by giving medication. With the use of the newer
drugs, they feel they finally have found a key, and they feel frustrated when
that key is removed from their hands. However, there are still many patients
who do not respond to any of the psychotropics and who have side-effects from
these medications. Such patients should be allowed to refuse these drugs.

Problem Areas in the
Right to Refuse Treatment

Competency to Refuse

Roth, Meisel, and Lidz (1977) have suggested that patients' competency to
decide on their treatment should be evaluated at the time of the commitment.
The one problem with that is the fact that patients' competency may change as
treatment progresses. In the state of Utah, however, a person is still deemed
to be incompetent if he is sufficiently mentally ill to be in need of involuntary
hospitalization and is so committed. As an incompetent in Utah, then, he can
be given medication against his will (Lebegue and Clark, 1981).

There may be an argument, especially in the *parens patria* approach,
that if a person is so mentally ill at the time she is involuntarily committed

(that is, she does not wish to go to the hospital but the judge deems her to be sufficiently seriously mentally ill that she requires hospitalization), then the judge in effect is saying to the patient, "You are not competent to decide your treatment, and I will impose the will of the state upon you by putting you in the hospital against your will, because you are dangerous, because you are mentally ill, and because you require hospitalization for treatment." Thus, the judge is saying that the patient is not competent to make the decision about her treatment, including the requirement for hospitalization and possibly medication.

The Least Restrictive Alternative

Arguments have been made that the right to the least restrictive alternative of treatment includes not only the geographical location (for example, a halfway house is less restrictive than a hospital, and outpatient treatment is less restrictive than any confinement) but also the type of treatment administered. The use of psychotherapy may be less restrictive than the use of medication, or medication that lasts only for a few hours may be less restrictive than an injection of medication that lasts for two weeks. Following the logic of that argument, one might say that, if a person is given the least restrictive treatment translated from geography to medication, one also can translate competency for treatment from the geography to the medication. A person who is not competent to decide that he needs to be in a hospital, and is so committed against his will by the judge, may also be deemed not to be competent to make the decision about his medication for treatment.

Choice of Medication

In a similar way, the doctor who has the patient for treatment may not be arbitrary in her selection of medication for treatment. She must provide medication on the basis of clinical experience, medical effectiveness, and psychiatrically accepted standards. An example of deviation from these standards occurred in a recent instance involving a patient who complained that because he would not take the medication prescribed he was seen by his psychiatrist as a person who was refusing treatment. When examined, he said he was not refusing treatment but only the particular medication that his doctor wished to give him. When asked what that medication was, he said it was a newer form of injectable tranquilizer that he did not wish to take because his roommate had developed the "shakes" and he did not want to have similar symptoms. When asked what he would take, he named an older psychotropic medicaion that he said he had used previously with success and without the unwanted side-effect he had observed in his roommate. It seemed logical that the patient should be treated with the more comfortable, familiar, and safer medication. When asked whether he discussed this with his doctor, he acknowledged that he had and that his doctor's attitude was "no one is going to tell me how to practice medicine!" When the doctor was approached about this choice of medication by an unbiased appointed psychiatrist, a similar arrogant response was received. Only the authority of the judge overcame the arrogance of the treating psychiatrist, who was ordered to give the patient the safer medication that he would accept. In all fairness, the psychiatrist did indicate that the patient was manipulating and that he later would refuse the other tranquilizer as well. In order to avoid the "ping-ponging" threatened by such a move, the judge ordered the patient to take the medication he wished to have but stated that if he refused that medication then the doctor was at liberty to prescribe the type of medication she felt would be most helpful.

Another abuse of the use of medication has originated from the need to study the effects of certain types of newer medication and the desire of some researchers to conduct research on patients, even against their will. A number of patients have complained that they were taking medication, not because it was specific for their problems, but because the doctor was conducting a research project and required their use of the medication she wished to give. When they refused to take the medication, she continued with it, saying that she was the doctor and would prescribe whatever she felt was necessary. Again, in this case, the judge overruled the research efforts of the psychiatrist, indicating that she was to prescribe acceptable medications in acceptable dosages and not conduct research on newer medications with patients who were unwilling to be involved in the research program.

Thus, it appears that the right to refuse treatment is essentially a right to refuse medication that may be harmful to the patient. It makes good sense that when a judge imposes the rule of patients' rights, that the treating physician should be more precise and more aware of the treatment modalities used with particular patients.

Obligation to Provide Adequate Treatment

Because providing adequate treatment (and its subsidiary, the right to refuse unwanted medication) may pose a hardship on hospitals and physicians who are burdened with excessive numbers of patients or inadequate resources, the APA Task Force (1977) addressed this issue. They stated,

> The recognition and definition of a right to adequate care and treatment for the patient implies that society has a duty to both implement and enforce this right. Psychiatrists responsible for public and other mental health services often are assigned the duty of treating patients legally committed to their care, whereas the actual facilities and staff resources supplied by society are simply inadequate

to the task. This has placed an unfair and unjust burden on the psychiatrists. For this reason we encourage psychiatrists to document and inform their employers, community and professional organizations about inadequate resources for the care and treatment of their patients. Physicians are dependent on society, through its agencies, for the provision of adequate funds and other resources necessary to meet their moral and medical responsibilities. It would be unjust and unreasonable for courts to hold psychiatrists personally and individually responsible for resource deficiencies that are actually the responsibility of society. [p. 355]

The statement of the Task Force certainly holds true for all mental health professionals, and not psychiatrists alone, in this complex sphere of conflicts.

Conclusions and Remaining Topics of Discussion

The debate is far from over. The pivotal issue of the right to treatment versus the right to refuse treatment involves a number of other major concepts relative to the doctor–patient relationship. These include the individual integrity of the patient, confidentiality, privileged communications between patient and doctor, and, most importantly, informed consent to any procedure or treatment that is given to the patient. Patients must be informed about treatment, what it will do, what it will not do, and what harmful effects it may have, as well as its beneficial intent. Furthermore, patients must be told what alternatives of treatment are available and what the consequences of these alternatives may be. Patients who are competent to give consent must be allowed to have the opportunity to discuss with the doctors and other mental health professionals the treatment plans that are offered. Treatment must not be forced upon a patient unless he becomes an "emergency" such that he or others may be hurt if he is not properly treated, or unless he is incompetent to give his consent and has a guardian appointed who will give consent for him.

One of the central issues in the debate appears to be the so-called "medical model" of treatment. Adhering to the medical model brings out a number of positive as well as negative points. Physicians have been trained to treat illness and to respect the patient's pain and suffering. They also have learned to utilize informed consent (which had its origin in medicine and surgery) and not to batter or assault the patient against his will. The medical model also implies a physiological or biological origin to a number of maladies and the use of medication or physical therapies or treatments for such illnesses.

On the other hand, the nonmedical model of mental disorder implies no illness but merely a maladjustment to society or a difficulty in coping with life's stresses. Here the model is therapy without medication, especially if a biological origin is not recognized.

One of the difficulties of the medical model is the authoritarian attitude adopted by a number of physicians who believe they know better than the patient what is good for the patient. Patients' groups and former-patients' groups have resented this arbitrary, authoritative, and occasionally arrogant attitude of psychiatrists, who have imposed their will upon patients. This argument comes to a focus most clearly in the area of the right to refuse medication. Some patients believe they know what is best for them, irrespective of the physician's training and experience. Many will point to the model established by Norman Cousins in his experience in "An Anatomy of an Illness as Seen by the Patient" (1976). In his paper (now expanded to a best-selling book), Cousins notes that he was terminally ill and hope was dim for his recovery by traditional methods of treatment, even by highly qualified, competent physicians. He asked whether he could help the doctors in their efforts to treat him. He was allowed to make decisions about the care and treatment of his body and his illness in a way that was unorthodox, but not totally illogical. He soon recovered. His claim to be the luckiest patient alive was based, he said, not on the fact that he lived, but on the fact that he had a doctor who would listen to him.

The examples discussed earlier in this chapter relate to the medical model of treatment and involve the physician who has the medical responsibility for prescribing medications and monitoring their use. Certainly the psychiatric nurse and other mental health professionals working on the treatment team share in the decision making regarding the maintenance of various forms of treatment, including medication. If medication is not allowed, it appears that the treatment team will need to develop specific therapeutic modalities of a nonmedical nature for the patient within their care.

Thus, it is important for all professionals working in the mental health area to listen to the patient and, to the extent possible, allow the patient to participate in the decision making in her own treatment. These are essential ingredients to a proper attitude of care and treatment of mentally ill patients in this era of increasingly expanding patients' rights.

References

American Psychiatric Association. Report of the Task Force on the Right to Adequate Care and Treatment for the Mentally Ill and Mentally Retarded. *American Journal of Psychiatry, 134*:3, March 1977, pp. 354–355.

Cousins, N. Anatomy of an Illness as Perceived by the Patient. *The New England Journal of Medicine*, December 23, 1976, 1458–1463.

Lebegue, B., & Clark, L. D. Incompetence to Refuse Treatment: A Necessary Condition for Civil Commitment. *American Journal of Psychiatry, 138*:8, August 1981, 1075–1077.

In Re: Fussa, Paul. 46912, Hennepin County, Minnesota, June 14, 1976.

In Re: Lundquist, Cleo. 140151, Ramsey County, Minnesota, April 30, 1976.

Price v. Sheppard. 239 NW 2d 905, Minn., 1976.

Rachlin, S. One Right Too Many. *Bulletin of the American Academy of Psychiatry and the Law, 3*:2, 1975, 99.

Rachlin, S. Civil Commitment, Parens Patriae, and the Right to Refuse Treatment. *The American Journal of Forensic Psychiatry, 1,* July 1979, 174–189.

Rennie v. Klein. 462 F. Supp. 1131 D.N.J., 1979.

Rogers v. Okin. 478 F. Supp. 1342, D. Mass., 1979.

Roth, L., Meisel, A., and Lidz, C. W. et al., Tests of Competency to Consent to Treatment, *American Journal of Psychiatry, 134,* 1977, 279–284.

Winters v. Miller. 446 F. 2d, 65 (2nd Cir.), 404 U.S. 985, 1971.

Chapter 6

Rights of Treaters

Patients' Rights versus Treaters' Rights

With all due concern for the rights of patients, many mental health professionals have asked, "What are the rights of those who treat the patients?" Therapists and all mental health professionals are concerned that they will be inexorably forced into the middle of an ever-changing situation which would place the blame for damage to patients directly upon them. For example, clinicians clearly are aware that their inability to predict dangerousness has led to lawsuits against them and the hospitals when patients were discharged and then went on to hurt someone or to commit suicide. They do not wish to be forced to treat a patient in a manner contrary to their training and therapeutic experience. Therapists have expressed considerable concern over such concepts as "least restrictive alternative," "right to refuse treatment," and "commitment to outpatient treatment." They recognize there is no control for treating in the community a person whom they feel should be hospitalized. They also feel that it would be inappropriate to treat a schizophrenic without psychotropic medication when that person is subject to the ravages of his illness, which include frightening hallucinations and provocative delusions. They are concerned about elderly psychotic patients who deteriorate when their illness controls their behavior and their doctors are prevented by court order to intervene medically. They worry about treating a person in a less restrictive alternative when that person, in their opinion, is likely to become violent under certain clinical conditions over which they have little or no control. Most are not particularly concerned about the law, but they are concerned about the welfare of their patients. They feel frustrated and impotent at the court's order to withhold medication from a competent person who refuses his medication. They wonder who is responsible for treating the patient when the court ties their hands. Clinicians have been concerned about getting sued for violating patients' rights and have felt the stronger advocacy has been with the patients rather than the professionals. They have expressed their concern that they are getting short-changed in this battle of rights.

When patients are allowed to refuse medication that admittedly has the effect of controlling their behavior, nurses and other professional staff have complained that patients have become violent, have disrupted ward procedure, and have injured staff and other patients. This was especially the concern in the Boston State Hospital case of *Rogers* v. *Okin* (1979), where patients were allowed to discontinue their medication through court injunction and became more aggressive and violent in the wards. The injunction resulted in an increase in the use of restraints to help control violent behavior by patients. Staff morale was lowered, and professional staff feared for their safety. Nurses have asked whether they have the right to restrain patients who show signs of disruptive behavior, even though they have not actually harmed anyone. They have asserted their right to be free from the harmful behavior of their patients, while patients' civil rights are maintained within the hospital.

Thus, restraints, medication, control of behavior, and movement of patients are all concerns of mental health professionals, concerns that were once taken for granted as part of the treatment program. What rights do the treating professionals have in the current state of transition?

Collins' Analysis

Perhaps the most comprehensive analysis of this concern is presented by Dr. Dean Collins (1980), a psychiatrist at the Menninger Clinic. He lists several rights of mental health professionals, primarily concerned with the psychiatrist treating involuntarily committed patients. He says, "I speak as a psychiatrist, but the principles for my profession surely have correlates in the other mental health professions." (p. 293).

1. *The right to form an independent opinion.* Surely this is an obligation the professional has to the patient rather than a right; but Dr. Collins is concerned particularly with the patient who diagnoses himself. The psychiatrist or mental health professional should not be forced to give in to the demands of the patient if they are contrary to the clinical judgment of the therapist.

2. *The right to define personal and professional limitations.* This is also an obligation or a duty the professional owes to her patient. Dr. Collins, however, states this principle not as a duty but as a right of the professional not to be forced by the patient or other persons to exceed her professional or personal limits. The clinician should know what she is able to do professionally and must retain the right to refuse to exceed her limits and to aid the patient

by helping to find a clinician who has the expertise required to meet the patient's request.

3. *The right to formulate a treatment plan that is anticipated to be effective in achieving explicit goals.* The cases that have developed in patients' rights have specified this principle as a duty owed to the patient by the professional. This may be more a matter of a patient's right than a treater's right, but Dr. Collins again asserts that neither patients nor outside agencies should be responsible for outlining a treatment plan that forces the therapist to follow outside guidelines for treatment rather than the clinician's own best judgment. An example is the therapist's recommending hospitalization rather than outpatient treatment, even with resistance from the patient, when the therapist believes the hospital is a necessary part of the treatment plan for that particular patient.

4. *The right to define the characteristics of the clinical setting that will best serve the purpose of goal achievement.* Again, this appears to be an obligation the treater owes to the patient in providing the best possible treatment available under the circumstances. However, Dr. Collins insists that it is the right or duty of the professional and not of the patient or other outside agencies to enforce a clinical setting that is consistent with the achievement of treatment goals as outlined by the therapist. His major concern is that of making the psychiatric hospital an extension of the jail. He is concerned that strict detention techniques may deter, rather than enhance, the growth of the patient in the hospital. He concludes that the professional retains the right "to define the characteristics that would best serve clinical purposes and to oppose encroachment upon the fulfillment of those purposes by other considerations" (p. 294).

5. *The right to consult with colleagues.* This seems very clearly to be a duty the professional owes the patient if consultation is required to treat the patient in the most effective manner. Dr. Collins, however, notes the fact that confidentiality between therapist and patient could keep the therapist from consulting with colleagues if the patient refuses to give permission to share information with others. Dr. Collins very properly notes that confidentiality should never preclude "the freedom of the professional to consult with a colleague. He must not be shackled by explicit or implicit vows of secrecy to such an extent that he cannot consult other professionals regarding his judgment and assessment of cases" (Collins, 1980, p. 294).

6. *The right to maintain undisclosed her observations, thoughts, formulations, and predictions about the patient.* This right has been spelled out very clearly as a duty of the therapist to her patient. However, Dr. Collins very properly notes that occasionally the treater will be pressured by law or other forces to reveal information about her patients that she may choose not to disclose. Dr. Collins is most concerned here about the clinician's notes

about the patient; her hypotheses, formulations, and predictions. Here we encounter the concept of the Tarasoff decision (*Tarasoff* v. *The Regents of the University of California*, 1974), which mandates therapists to warn or protect third parties who may be victims of the violence of their patients. After careful consideration, the Tarasoff decision makes good sense if the therapist is reasonably certain that her patient will harm a third person. The therapist should take steps to protect the life of the third party, just as she would take appropriate steps to save the life of her patient if the patient was threatening to commit suicide. Tarasoff, however, covers only violence to third parties, not suicidal attempts.

7. *The right to terminate responsibility for the treatment and care of a patient upon giving reasonable notification and assistance in finding other professional services.* This is not only a right of the professional, but a very clear obligation the professional has both to his patient and to himself. No therapist ever ought to be put in such a position that he is forced to treat a patient inadequately according to his standards. If a court insists that a patient is not to receive medication and yet is to remain on a specific ward in a particular hospital, then the doctor in charge should have alternate options for helping to control the person's behavior if he becomes violent. No case has emerged yet that has precluded the use of medication in bona fide emergencies. The professional has a duty to medicate the patient who has lost control and requires medication because of the emergency situation. However, if such alternate methods of treatment are not available and the therapist's or his colleagues' lives or safety are in jeopardy because of the court's orders for treatment, the therapist has several options available:

      a. The therapist could bring the problem directly to the judge and obtain a clarification of the order and reasonable options to follow in the event of an emergency.

      b. The therapist may seclude, restrain, or isolate the patient who is potentially violent or harmful, to avoid violence until further clarification by the court.

      c. The therapist may resign, may leave the hospital, and leave to others the treatment of such an "impossible" patient in a difficult situation. They also may choose this option to leave. Fortunately there have not been many such instances.

However, less drastic situations may arise in which a therapist may decide that he no longer wishes to continue treating a patient or believes that his continuing to treat a patient is not in the patient's best interest nor in the therapist's personal best interest. The therapist always should have the option to refer that patient to other qualified, competent therapists in the community. To avoid a charge of abandonment, the therapist should give the patient the names of three competent therapists to whom the patient may go for follow-up treatment. To avoid difficulty in communication or credibili, statements, the therapist should document his communication to the patie by sending a certified letter, with return receipt, to the patient indicating that he will no longer assume responsibility for the patient's medical care after 30 days; and within the thirty days, if the patient has difficulty reaching a follow-up therapist or difficulty obtaining treatment from one of the referrals, then the therapist will give three other names, but under no circumstances will continue to treat the patient after a specified date. This sets a limitation for the patient that is reasonable and within the standard of care in the community.

Treater's Right to Give Adequate Care

It is extremely important as a general principle for a therapist not to be put in the position of treating a patient inadequately, even if it appears to be mandated by some other agency, the court, or even the patient herself according to her wishes or demands. The therapist is the one who must make the decision about treatment in terms of modality, setting, goals, and so on. He should do this whenever possible with the direct participation of the patient, but must not be forced by the patient to treat her inadequately. If a compromise attempt is made that fails, the therapist, not the patient, will be the one who is held professionally responsible and who may be sued for failing to meet the standards of care in the community.

Treffert & Crajeck (1976) compared the commitment statutes in various states with what is called a "model commitment statute" and outlined what they have called treaters' rights:

> The statute should specify that the treater also has specific rights—to use the customary and usual treatments or procedures in a reasonable and appropriate manner in an effort to ameliorate the conditions that led to the patient's commitment, to use emergency procedures in life threatening situations, and to curtail specified patients' rights (personal possessions, visitors, and so forth) if necessary for proper treatment—but only after documented administrative review. [p. 290]

An analysis of Treffert & Crajeck's treatment rights addition to the model commitment statute indicates that these rights are really obligations to the patient. Treaters can always use emergency procedures in life-threatening situations. This does not have to be spelled out as a treater's right. All cases have allowed emergency treatment, especially when people's lives are in jeopardy. The curtailing of specified patients' rights by treaters when necessary for proper treatment is a highly controversial area that needs further discussion. Certainly, patients who are out on pass should not be allowed to bring marijuana, sharp knives, or other dangerous instruments onto the wards where highly disturbed patients may damage themselves. The question is, how should returning patients be prevented from doing this? Should each patient who returns from pass automatically be stripped and searched? Should only those suspicious patients who have a history of bringing contraband onto the wards be searched? Should no one be searched? The arguments have raged on both sides of the question in malpractice suits against hospitals. Plaintiffs' attorneys have argued vehemently that hospitals are negligent for allowing patients to bring contraband onto the wards and that, if necessary, every patient should be strip-searched before returning. Defense lawyers for the hospitals and also civil rights attorneys, upholding the rights of patients, abhor such searches and argue that only those people who are likely to bring contraband onto the ward should be searched, and only with permission of the patient, the treating physician, and/or the hospital administration.

Should all patients who become disturbed be restrained or locked up in order to prevent violence? If the staff does not restrain a patient who is then allowed to harm someone by acting out his internal conflicts through violence, the hospital may be sued in tort by the victim of the unprovoked attack. The argument will be that the staff did not protect adequately the innocent and injured party by necessarily and properly restraining the violent person. The argument on the other side will dictate that patients are not to be restrained in anticipation of their becoming violent, because no one can predict their dangerousness and they must be allowed to be unrestrained at least until they demonstrate that they are violent.

Hospital staff have great difficulty with these questions, and perhaps the more practical approach is one that allows several alternatives to either full restraint or free rein of violent behavior. One-on-one therapy, for example, is often very calming to a potentially disturbed person whose early upset may be noted long before violence ensues. Talking the patient down is a very common form of therapy that is utilized in most well-staffed hospitals. If there are insufficient staff people for such treatment, then restraint may be required until adequate staff can be obtained or until further options are developed. No patient should be allowed free rein for violent behavior, and yet numbers of patients should not be restrained indiscriminately in order to avoid anticipated violent behavior.

The staff should have the right to exercise its discretion, after proper training and appropriate experience, in handling potentially violent patients by a number of means—including individual counseling, group counseling, isolation, separation, partial restraint—before full restraint or involuntary injection of medication is utilized.

The Right of Disclosure

Another question that is raised often by nursing staff in large mental hospitals involves the disclosure of information about a patient's condition. Who has the right to know how a person is doing? Should no information be given? Specific guidelines for disclosure of information are necessary in treating the mentally ill. The treatment team should designate one person to disclose information under carefully controlled guidelines. Others on the treatment team can state that they are not permitted to give information about the patient, but that the inquirer may contact the team member who is responsible for this. This doctor then has the option of disclosing the information or not, depending on her judgment with respect to the patient. For the most part, patients must give informed consent, either orally or in writing, for disclosure of information. Sometimes the designated discloser does not wish to disclose the information, even though the patient gives permission. Here, an administrative decision may be required by the hospital authority that supervises the treatment team. It is always safer for the staff not to disclose any information about a patient without first consulting the designated person who is responsible for such disclosures. Any conflicts that arise always should be referred to the hospital administration and ultimately to the hospital attorney.

The Right to Terminate Treatment

Up to this point, we have discussed how the rights of professionals are intimately intertwined with the obligations the mental health professionals have for the patients. All treaters are obligated to provide adequate treatment according to guidelines determined by community standards and enforced and applied by the practitioners. The rights of the mental health professionals involve their autonomy in not being forced to treat a person in a manner they consider to be inappropriate, unethical, or inadequate. They also have rights of redress of grievance, as do patients, which they may exercise by turning to the hospital attorney or to their own attorney and, ultimately, to the courts, to resolve questions conflicts.

Unlike involuntarily committed mental patients, however, mental health professionals have the option to resign or to leave their positions if they feel forced to treat a patient in a way that is antithetical to their professional or personal beliefs. That right always remains, so no attempt should be made to take it away. Only when a particular psychiatrist, psychologist, nurse, social worker, or counselor is the only professional within a 100-mile radius and no reasonable referral source exists should the professional then assume responsibility for treating the patient even if she wishes not to do so. However, every effort should be made to find alternative treatment resources. In situations of this type, where there is one professional who is the "last resort" or if it involves the state hospital beyond which the patient cannot go, the rights of the professional should be considered thoroughly, since the therapist does not have the option to abandon the patient without proper referral treatment sources.

General Legal Guidelines

The following list of suggestions may be helpful in dealing with some of the changes that have occurred in the legal regulation of mental health practice.

1. Be certain to define concepts that are utilized in the treatment of the patient. This is especially true of "dangerousness," "mental illness," and other concepts used to discuss particular patients and is especially important when testifying in court. It is important to be certain the judge knows what the professional means when he uses such words as "dangerous" or "incompetent" or uses various other labels to define, diagnose, or describe a patient.

2. In the event of an emergency within the hospital, the mental health professional should treat the patient as an emergency and not be overly concerned about legal matters. Usually the emergency doctrine will override legal principles that apply to normal situations. It may be important to obtain a second opinion from a respected colleague or other mental health professional confirming that this is a bona fide emergency situation (see Chapter 7). From a medical point of view it is essential to administer the treatment when necessary and not to stand by passively and allow the patient to harm himself or someone else. In the event of an emergency, a patient's medical needs outweigh his legal rights. This concept has been accepted in all emergency treatment doctrines.

3. When treating a patient who refuses particular types of treatment, including medication, it is important to
    a. Listen to the patient to hear what his concerns are
    b. Allow the patient, to the extent possible within the limits of his illness, to participate in the decision making about his own treatment

4. The mental health professional working in a hospital would be well advised to work closely either with the hospital attorney or the attorney who advises on hospital treatment of psychiatric patients. If the attorney is not available or not helpful in particular cases, the therapist should consult the attorney representing the wishes of the patient.

The last recommendation may seem strange or unusual to some, but it is quite important and in keeping with Kopolow's (1976) doctrine of the mental health professional as the true advocate for the patient. All helpers must learn to work together with the patient and her attorney in order to provide the highest quality of care while upholding the legal rights of the patient. When the two are in conflict, then it is essential to provide for the patient's needs. Let the patient's attorney advocate the patient's wants and develop the patient's rights. Each professional has a different role with respect to the care of the patient. Treaters must be advocates, as mental health professionals, for the best medical interest of the patient while at the same time observing her civil rights, or at least not abusing them. However, therapists also must not uphold the patient's rights to the point where the patient is harmed medically.

Therapists must balance their concerns about the rights of treaters with the greater obligation of the treater to the patient. If good, professional, mental health care is given the patient, there should be no difficulty upholding her civil rights. It is not appropriate for treaters to argue for treaters' rights; rather, they should advocate patients' rights, which are served best when treaters have the freedom to practice their profession in the most effective manner.

References

Collins, D. T. The Rights of Mental Health Professionals. *Bulletin of the Menninger Clinic, 44*:3, 1980, 291–295.

Kopolow, L. Patients' Rights and the Psychiatrists' Dilemma. *Bulletin of the American Academy of Psychiatry and the Law,* 1976, 4:3, 197–203.

Rogers v. Okin. 478 F. Supp. 1342, D. Mass., 1979.

Tarasoff v. The Regents of the University of California et al., 529 P. 2d 553 Calif., 1974.

Treffert, D. A., & Crajeck, D. W. In Search of a Commitment Statute. *Psychiatric Annals,* June 1976, 283–294.

Chapter 7

Psychiatric Emergencies: The Management of Violent and Suicidal Patients

Emergency medicine has become an established specialty of medicine. Fellowship programs and residencies are geared toward the management of the emergency medical patient. Physicians now are specializing in emergency medical work and have contracted to run the emergency rooms of various hospitals. Emergency psychiatry, however, has not been developed as formally, but various principles and guidelines have been established to aid the practitioner in the management of bona fide psychiatric emergencies.

Definition of Emergency and the Proper Response to It

Psychiatric emergencies may occur either in the community, from which the patient then is brought to the emergency room of the hospital, or they may occur in the psychiatric or general hospital and require immediate attention. The emergencies include suicidal behavior, violent or homicidal behavior, acute withdrawal from barbiturates or methamphetamines, delirium tremens following withdrawal of alcohol, and panic reactions. Psychiatric conditions that may require emergency psychiatric care include acute mania, agitated depression, aggressive forms of catatonic schizophrenia, and acute paranoid states.

The responsibility of the professional is to care for the acute emergency by administering immediate treatment. With the advent of newer laws regulating psychiatric and mental health practice, many clinicians are concerned about involuntarily medicating individuals or treating a patient who is reluctant to be treated. It should be noted that, in bona fide emergency situations, all patients need immediate medical and psychiatric attention and should not be deprived of adequate treatment because of undue concern for laws or regulations that prohibit medical intrusion in nonemergency situations. In all jurisdictions, emergency conditions override these legal regulations. The primary concern is for the life and welfare of the patient. It is often helpful subsequently for the therapist to obtain consultation from a respected colleague to confirm the existence of the emergency. The patient may require injection, seclusion, restraint, or all three. If seclusion or restraint is administered, then one-to-one observation should be given until the emergency subsides.

If the patient is psychotic, terrified, or otherwise unable to exhibit rational thought or behavior, he may be presumed to be incompetent to give rational consent to treatment. In that case the treater should administer emergency treatment with the understanding that if the patient were rational he would give consent for such treatment. This is called "presumed consent" in the law. If a family member is present or available, vicarious consent should be given by the next-of-kin or the relative who can give proper consent for the patient.

By no means should the involuntary treatment extend beyond the period of the emergency. It is especially important to have careful monitoring of the person involved in the emergency treatment. Patients should not be left in restraints or seclusion for 24 hours before being checked. They should be checked every ten or fifteen minutes, until the emergency subsides. The restraints then should be removed gradually until the patient is able to resume normal liberties. The medication may be continued in order to avoid the recurrence of a panic state or a new emergency situation.

If the patient refuses to continue the medication, a due-process hearing with a judge should be requested to determine whether continued medication should be administered or whether the patient should be removed from the treatment regimen. It is important to have the judge or some duly authorized person make such a decision, in order to provide the patient with full due process of law and also to attach legal responsibility to the judge for subsequent behavior by the patient. If the clinician determines, without the authorization of a judge, that treatment will be continued after the emergency has ended and the patient refuses treatment, the clinician may be held in violation of the patient's civil rights to refuse treatment. If, however, the therapist, without the order of the judge, decides to withhold treatment when the patient refuses medication and the patient continues to act in a violent manner, harming either himself or someone else, the therapist may be held responsible for failing to give adequate treatment when it was necessary. Thus, it is wise, and especially important in these days of changing laws and interpretations of rules governing mental health practice, that the judge be called to provide due process to the patient and to assume legal responsibility for the subsequent behavior of the patient.

Many have been concerned about judicial intervention in medical decision making. Many physicians have felt threatened by the imposition of judicial authority in situations formerly managed exclusively by psychiatrists; however, the ever-changing laws and rules governing psychiatric practice mandated that this intervention occur to protect both patients and therapists.

Suicidal Behavior

With respect to suicidal behavior, the treater should evaluate the patient along the following guidelines:

1. Is the patient talking about killing himself?
2. Has the patient thought of particular ways of doing so?
3. Has the patient accumulated the necessary tools for completion of his suicidal intent?
4. Has the patient attempted suicide in the past?
5. Has the patient tried a minor form of suicide such as cutting his wrist slightly to see how it would feel when he cuts his throat? Has the patient taken several pills but not a sufficient number to kill himself as a practice or warm-up gesture?

This line of questioning is designed to determine how far beyond the mere thought of killing oneself the patient has gone. Many people think and speak about killing themselves but have no firm intention of doing so. Evaluation of a person's *behavior* with respect to suicidal intent is the important consideration.

It is helpful to gather certain demographic information for use in analyzing suicidal behavior. Ascertain the age, sex, marital status, and occupational situation of the patient. It is well known, for example, that middle-aged males who are recently divorced, have recently lost their jobs, and who are alcoholic have a higher tendency toward suicide than males of the same age with more stable family and occupational history.

Another series of questions which may yield answers important to prediction involves recent events in a person's life that may precipitate depression and suicidal behavior.

Self-destructive behavior short of suicide, such as maiming, torturing, cutting, or starving one's self through neglect, is important in assessing future self-destructive behavior that could lead to emergency conditions.

Dangerousness

With respect to the concept of dangerousness to others, it should be remembered that psychiatric expertise is lacking in the prediction of such behavior. Clinicians can conclude that there is a high potential for violent behavior in two types of situations. The first is where the patient is imminently explosive and appears about to harm someone immediately. In the second, the patient has a history of violent behavior under the present clinical conditions (for example, the patient is a 34-year-old, paranoid schizophrenic male who has a history of becoming violent when he stops taking his psychotropic medication, drinks alcohol to excess, and gets into arguments with other men). Other predictions of violent behavior, however, become less reliable over time. For example, the studies of Monahan (1981) have shown that the reliability and validity of predicting future violent behavior may be fairly good on the short-term basis but not good over a long period of time. There is no particular time limit that is designated, but it appears through clinical experience that reasonably accurate prediction may be limited to a few hours or a few days and probably becomes less reliable after that.

Thus it is important for the clinician not to put herself in the position of making predictions about violent behavior or dangerousness beyond a certain time and out of the context of clinical situations. This is especially true when determining commitability of a patient and time for release of a person who had been deemed mentally ill and dangerous by the court or the reviewing authority. (Please refer to the discussions of definitions of dangerousness and applicability to clinical situations in Chapter 3.)

Emergency Psychiatric Consultations in Liaison with Other Professionals

In a general hospital, the psychiatrist often is called upon by her medical and surgical colleagues to evaluate patients who are considered in need of surgical or medical procedures which they refuse. One of the most common situations is exemplified by that of an elderly woman who had diabetes mellitus with complications including gangrene of one of her lower extremities. The surgeons deemed it necessary for her to have an amputation in order to save her life. The woman, however, did not wish to have her leg removed and preferred to allow the gangrene to proceed, even under the knowledge that it could lead to her death. The surgeons, frustrated in their therapeutic efforts, turned to the psychiatrist for consultation of the patient's competency to make decisions about her treatment.

Quite often the patient is competent to make the decision and there is frustration on the part of both the psychiatrist and the surgeon. At other times the patient is clearly incompetent; in such an event, a guardian may be appointed or the judge may determine that the operation should proceed. Sometimes there is insufficient time to contact the judge, so a determination of incompetency on an emergency basis has to be made and the operation performed. In those cases, next-of-kin or family should be involved to aid in the decision making. When the family is not available or there is no family, then the doctors may have to make an emergency decision at the time and proceed with the life-saving operation.

If the patient is competent and decides not to have the operation, then the surgeon should not proceed or she may be subject to an assault-and-battery suit by the patient. The patient has a right to die if she is competent to decide that for herself. Often, however, the patient becomes so physically ill and debilitated or delirious with infection that though once competent she becomes incompetent. It is possible that the operation should then proceed.

In the event there is time to adjudicate the matter, the patient should be brought before a judge to determine whether she is competent to make the decision about her own treatment. A psychiatric consultation should be obtained as part of good medical care and also to meet the standard of care in the community. If the judge determines the patient is competent, then the decision of the judge protects the decision of the patient and the liability of the treating physicians. Under no circumstances should the surgeon proceed to operate on such a patient if the patient refuses treatment.

Another legally sticky situation that arises in liaison psychiatry involves the seriously medically ill person who has a psychiatric illness as well and may pose a threat of suicide or homicide while on the medical or surgical floor. Questions may arise regarding transfer of the patient to a psychiatric floor, though he may require continued surgical and medical treatment, even with intravenous fluids and other machinery attached to his body. The decision here is primarily a medical one, to be made in conjunction with psychiatric consultation. The priority of treatment rests with the severity of the medical illness and the need for medical–surgical nursing care and treatment as compared with the severity of the psychiatric illness and the threat posed to the patient or others if he is not transferred to a more secure psychiatric ward. The decision has to be a joint one that is based on the facilities available for providing security to the psychiatric patient, who must remain on a medical–surgical ward to receive either postoperative care or other medical–surgical procedures not available on the psychiatric floor. On the other hand, the patient may be transferred to the psychiatric ward if his threat of violence due to his psychotic illness is so great that secure facilities are not available on the medical floor to protect the life of the patient or the safety of others. Medical–surgical nursing care may have to be transferred to the psychiatric floor if the priority is determined to be the treatment of the psychosis rather than the medical or surgical illness. Sometimes these are very difficult problems that cannot be resolved easily. Cases have emerged in which the patient was not transferred to the psychiatric floor and was able to jump out a window that was not properly secured, which it would have been on the psychiatric floor. Other cases have arisen where such patients have become violent to nursing staff or to other patients. Some patients, in their delirium, have harmed themselves because of inadequate observation.

On the other hand, the decision to transfer such a patient to the psychiatric floor may mean a decrease in the intensity of his medical–surgical treatment, which may result in his not receiving proper medical care. Although this has happened in a few cases, it is much more likely that proper nursing care and medical treatment can be administered on a secure psychiatric floor. Only in a few, very select illnesses requiring exotic machinery and specialized nursing care will the patient not be transferred to psychiatry; however, in those cases the patient is usually not in a physical condition to become violent to himself or others. If the patient is not able to be transferred to a psychiatric floor, then one-to-one observation or special nursing care with frequent psychiatric visits may be implemented.

Another example is the delirious patient who, following surgery, may pose a threat of harm to himself or others because of his psychotic condition. Often these patients may be managed on the medical or surgical floor, but the psychiatric consultant should be available for regular and frequent consultation regarding restraint, seclusion, and/or medication.

In all these situations, the nurse caring for the patient has a primary responsibility to be certain that the patient does not harm himself or others. The nurse must keep the psychiatrist and the treating physician informed at all times about the mental state of the patient, as observed through his behavior, his words, and his emotional condition. Such patients may pose an emergency for the treatment team, so they must be carefully observed for sudden changes in their condition.

Questions of Delegated Responsibility

Often the attending physician or the psychiatric consultant writes a PRN (*pro re nata;* "as needed") order for the nurses to restrain, seclude, or medicate a patient if she shows changes in her demeanor or behavior. Courts have questioned the advisability of such PRN orders, wherein the primary responsibility is shifted from the physician to the nurse caring for the patient. It may be a better situation for the nurse to inform the physician of the immediate change in the patient, proceed to treat in order to avoid catastrophe, but be certain the physician is informed and comes to see the patient to confirm or revise the orders.

This particular issue hits on the very controversial concern of the professional responsibility of the nurse with respect to the physician. Does the nurse have independent professional responsibility for the care of the patient, or is the nurse dependent upon the doctor's orders with respect to preventing emergency situations from arising? Traditionally, the nurse has been seen in the courts as following the orders of the physician and keeping the physician informed regarding changes in the patient. More recently, nurses have proclaimed they have an independent responsibility to the patient and may at times assume the authority to treat emergency conditions, even those not covered by physicians' orders. The law is unclear at this point regarding such behavior. If the nurse exercises good judgment and the result is favorable to the patient, the court will uphold the decision. If, however, the nurse decides to treat the patient as an emergency beyond the orders given by the physician, with no new orders to follow, and a bad result occurs, the court may look unfavorably upon the independent action of the nurse. Here, it becomes a matter of teamwork between the nurse and physician to determine authority to treat in an emergency.

In such situations in hospitals, even administrators may be deemed liable if an untoward result occurs, since the head of the department or the administrator of the hospital is held responsible for training physicians and staff in the care of emergencies and other situations. Guidelines should be developed for hospitals to use and to follow, and roles should be delineated for each staff member in the event of various emergencies and unexpected medical situations.

Not all results can be foreseen, anticipated, or even prevented; however, the courts will look to the diligence of the staff and the safety of the environment in which the patient is treated in determining whether negligence or malpractice has occurred. Such considerations will include the type of windows, use of safety screens, padding on sharp concrete corners, or other potentially dangerous conditions. Courts may ask such questions as, Should the window have been left open on the fifth floor of the hospital? Should all windows be sealed in the event a delirious patient runs amuck or deliberately intends to kill himself?

Emergency Management Techniques

In the management of the emergency psychiatric patient, various techniques may be utilized. The law will look to the least restrictive alternative and the one with the least permanent changes in the patient. Courts may vary on their interpretation of these two factors and especially in determining types of "intrusive" treatments. Each hospital should develop its own set of guidelines to determine which treatment modality will be used first in the event of an emergency situation, which ones next, and so on, up to the most restrictive for the patient. Initially, soft restraints may be needed, followed by the possibility of harder restraints or seclusion. The room should be stripped of all dangerous objects such as belts, razor blades, pens, pencils, knives, or other utensils that can be used for violent or self-destructive behavior. Medication may be injected if the patient's emergency condition warrants it. He may be in a manic state and will wear himself out if allowed to continue without medication, or he may be so psychotic as not to be rational and thus may harm himself trying to get out of the restraints. Other forms of less restrictive treatment methods include one-to-one talking therapy, hydrotherapy, or people-control therapy (keeping a person isolated from others by having staff members surround him and help him deal with his lack of internal controls). Person-to-person therapy works best when a person is not as irrational as the emergency patient may be. It may be considered inappropriate to inject a person with medication when a talking-down approach will work, even if there is insufficient staff available for such time-consuming treatment. (This does not include the usually decreased staff working at night.) Staff–patient ratios will be assessed by courts in such matters in determining quality of care and appropriateness of treatment modality.

Where once the hospital staff was able to care for an emergency in a purely clinical manner with some reasonable success, it now is deemed necessary to be aware of the civil rights of the patient and her right to a hearing to determine whether treatment given in such an emergency situation was appropriate or excessive. Thus, it is especially important to refine the emergency-management guidelines in each hospital and clinical setting. The law will continue to regulate mental health practice, even in emergencies. In two recent cases, the two judges differed in their definitions of an emergency. One called an emergency a sudden change in a patient's condition that could lead to harm to himself or others (*Rennie* v. *Klein*, 1979). In the other case, the judge deemed an emergency to exist only when the patient is so mentally ill and out of control that he physically harms himself or someone else (*Rogers* v. *Okin*, 1979). Most medical staff personnel will not wait for the physical violence to occur and will prevent such violence by instituting treatment before the emergency becomes a disaster. The important consideration here is for all medical and mental health professionals to be aware of the legal rights of patients, even in emergencies, and to act according to legally accepted guidelines.

References

Monahan, J. The Clinical Prediction of Violent Behavior. Rockville, Md.: National Institute of Mental Health, 1981.

Rennie v. Klein. 462 F. Supp. 1131 D.N.J., 1979.

Rogers v. Okin. 478 F. Supp. 1342 D. Mass., 1979.

Chapter 8
Malpractice Considerations

The Four D's of Malpractice

In every mental health profession there are guidelines to practice and standards of care that must be followed. Breaching the standard, or working below the standard of care, represents a form of negligence to the patient. In order to prove malpractice against any mental health professional, the plaintiff (the injured party) would have to show that the professional had a duty to the patient, that he breached his duty or was negligent, and that the patient was *damaged* as a *direct* result of the *dereliction* of *duty* to the patient. These are the four D's of a successful malpractice claim. If any of these four D's is absent or questionable, then so is the claim of malpractice. For example, sometimes there is a bad result but no negligence (dereliction) to account for the damage; here there is no malpractice.

The Professional's
Duties to the Patient

Before we can understand dereliction of duty, we must have some understanding of the duties of the professional. In mental health practice, the professional owes a duty of care to the patient in the following areas:

1. *The duty to do no harm (primum non nocere).* This is a general rule that the concern of the professional for the patient must be a beneficial one that does not result in harm or damage to the patient, whether intentional or unintentional.

2. *The duty to protect confidentiality.* This issue is discussed more in detail in Chapter 1 but is included here for completeness. The professional must not disclose information inappropriately about a patient if she has learned it in the course of treating him and if that disclosure may lead to harm to the patient. If the doctor, one of her agents, or other mental health

professionals or their agents working with the patient disclose information that ultimately results in damage to the patient, the patient may have a cause of action against that professional, either directly or through the professional's agent (the agency rule). If, for example, a psychiatrist's secretary reveals to an employer that one of his employees is a patient in her office, the patient may sue the psychiatrist if, as a result of that disclosure, he loses his job.

The agency rule is invoked for a number of reasons. The basic responsibility belongs to the physician, the psychiatrist, or the mental health professional, and not to her subordinates. She must counsel, teach, and train her employees not to divulge information inappropriately. That is her responsibility as a professional. A second reason that the professional, and not the secretary, will be sued is the "deep pockets" theory: The professional's malpractice insurance carries more liability insurance than does the secretary's. It would not pay the plaintiff to sue for damages where little or no money could be recovered.

3. *The duty to obtain informed consent.* This is owed to the patient by all mental health professionals. It should be obtained before administering treatment, especially treatment that may result in harm to the patient. Without such informed consent, the patient may accuse the therapist of assaulting or battering him. The therapist must have consent from the patient after giving proper information about the procedure; this is especially true for electroshock therapy, psychosurgery, and other physical procedures. More recently it also has included medication, especially psychotropic medication, which has such potential side-effects as tardive dyskinesia.

The mental health professional also should obtain informed consent before releasing records or information about a patient. Without obtaining the consent, the patient may be harmed by the release without knowing that the disclosure was made. This may be similar to the confidentiality situation just discussed, but it is more likely to fall in the category of releasing information to third parties, such as insurance companies, courts, attorneys, or others who request or mandate its release. (For more detailed discussion of the proper ways of handling these requests, see the section on disclosure of information in Chapter 2.)

Two other major reasons why psychiatrists and mental health professionals are sued, in addition to the three just discussed, are (1) because a patient has successfully committed suicide or become injured in an unsuccessful suicide attempt and (2) because the therapist has mishandled the transference relationship in the course of psychotherapy. (Other duties of mental health professionals, the dereliction of which has involved them in malpractice lawsuits, are discussed more completely by Dawidoff in his book, *The Malpractice of Psychiatrists* (1973), by Halleck in the section on malpractice in his book, *Law in the Practice of Psychiatry* (1980), and by Cohen in his text, *Malpractice, A Guide for Mental Health Professionals* (1979). The reader is referred to these three fine sources.)

Self-Destructive Behavior

The therapist's duty to do no harm to the patient includes an implied obligation in psychiatric treatment, especially in psychiatric hospitals, not to allow the patient to harm himself. It is presumed that both the involuntary commitment of a patient to a hospital and the voluntary admission of a patient to a hospital are accomplished at least in part because the patient is not only mentally ill but also potentially harmful to himself or others. It is the purpose of putting him in the hospital to prevent the tragedy of suicide or homicide from occurring. Hospitals are equipped with locked psychiatric wards with safety windows, quiet rooms, and seclusion to prevent such violent behavior. If it does occur in a hospital setting, there is presumed to have been a breakdown in security that led to the violent behavior and the ultimate damage.

It is this breakdown in security that will be scrutinized by the court in the event of a malpractice lawsuit. The court will want to determine if the hospital staff could have anticipated the result and if they should have provided the security to prevent it. Certainly, hospitals and mental health professionals cannot lock people up indefinitely out of fear that they will commit suicide. There have to be adequate guidelines and predictors of behavior that are followed in order to assess properly the condition of the patient and his likelihood for self-destructive behavior. The courts will look to the diligence of the staff's preventive treatment. Was there negligence in the management of the patient, or did the staff consider the possible self-destructive behavior and discuss alternative plans for treatment? The court will look to the progress notes, the nursing notes, the treatment plan, and the patient's response to treatment. It will look to comments made by the patient that might indicate his potential for self-destructive behavior, clues that may have been overlooked by the staff or not properly discussed. The court will look to the profile of the patient to see whether he is in the "high-risk" group for suicide. It also will look to see whether the treatment team obtained prior records that might have indicated a history or pattern of self-damaging or suicidal behavior.

Several cases have emerged with respect to suicidal behavior within hospital settings, with various results. In one typical case, a patient had been on a walk outdoors with several other patients and staff and had broken unexpectedly from the group, run across the street, and been hit by a car and killed. The hospital was found to be not liable for the patient's death, since there was no way the staff could anticipate or predict that such impulsive behavior would occur or that the damage would result.

Another typical case is the patient who jumps out of an upper-floor hospital window and dies or is severely damaged by the fall. The question usually focuses around the open window or the availability of the window to the patient, and whether the patient was self-destructive in a deliberate manner or confused that she did not realize that she was leaving the hospital by an upper floor. Sometimes the cause is the patient's panic, which results in her needing so badly to get out of the hospital that she cannot give it rational thought. The self-destructive behavior then may not be deliberate or intentional but may result from confusion, disorientation, delirium, or panic. In these cases the court will look to the location of the window, its accessibility to the patient, and the degree of external controls placed on the patient by the staff. It will look to consultation with psychiatrists and other mental health professionals and the question of transferring the patient to a more secure floor. It will look to the means of control and how it was instituted. Within the concept of the least restrictive alternative of treatment, the court will determine if the patient was given some help with her controls or was neglected by the clinicians in this aspect of her care.

In such cases, after the lawsuit has been filed, an expert witness usually is obtained to review the records to determine whether there was any way the staff could predict that the patient would react in a self-destructive way, either intentionally or accidentally. The expert would review the nursing notes, the doctor's progress notes, and the demographic data about the patient and determine (1) whether or not the treatment team should have known the patient was potentially self-destructive and (2) whether they should have instituted tighter controls or treated the patient in a manner that would be consistent with "the standards of care in that community."

It should be noted that the "standards of care in the community" are now general standards across the country and not limited to a particular community. There are, however, guidelines for various hospitals that may not pertain to other hospitals. For example, the treatment in a university hospital teaching center may be more specific than the standards in a country hospital far from a medical teaching center. However, the argument would be made that the therapists in the country hospital should consult with those professionals in a medical teaching center, if the need arises, to determine what further treatment would be necessary, including possible transfer to the medical center. Courts have determined that the standards of care are equalized by the speedy means of present-day communication, especially the telephone, and by the easy transferability of patients from one community to another. Thus, an expert witness from New York City, for example, may comment on the standard of care in Youngstown, Ohio or Helena, Montana.

The euphemism utilized for negligence by many experts is that the treatment fell below the standard of care in this particular situation. The expert is then obliged to give reasons why the patient should have been treated differently and why the self-destructive behavior should have been anticipated and prevented. As in all other malpractice claims, the four D's hold; that is; was the *damage* to the patient a *direct* result of the negligence or the *dereliction* of *duty* of the therapist? It must be determined, then, in order for the suicidal behavior to be deemed malpractice, that the therapist had a duty—which he fell short of meeting—and that this negligence directly caused the damage to the patient. Thus, it must be shown that the doctor or the mental health professional knew, or should have known, that the patient was suicidal. If he did not know, it was only through his negligence that he failed to ascertain the self-destructive behavior and therefore failed to treat it and properly prevent the damage to the patient.

In malpractice claims, as in most tort or injury suits, the statute of limitation is two years. This is not to say that the suit must be brought within two years of the last visit of the patient to the therapist; rather what this means is that the patient or his family must bring suit within two years of the time they noted the negligence and the damage. What the court must determine is when the two years began. Sometimes the two years do not begin for several years after the last visit, because the patient did not recognize for some time that the damage sustained was directly related to the type of treatment he received or did not receive.

Mishandling of the
Transference Relationship

The general legal principles just discussed for self-destructive behavior also hold true for suits stemming from a therapist's mishandling of the transference relationship during psychotherapy. This event may occur to any mental health professional conducting any form of psychotherapy with any patient. Most commonly it has occurred with male psychotherapists (psychiatrists and psychologists) treating female patients. In these cases the mishandling of the transference occurred through sexual behavior by the therapist toward the patient. The therapist may have claimed that the sexual involvement was consensual, or that it occurred after the treatment ended, or that it was separate from the treatment session. The therapist also has claimed that he could not help himself because:

1. He fell in love with the patient.
2. The patient was excessively seductive and he responded to her charms.
3. He believed that it was therapeutic for the patient to be involved sexually with him.

Consent

The consensual nature of the sexual behavior is not relevant to the claim made by the patient. Even if the patient agreed to the sexual behavior, the claim has been made successfully that the patient could not give true consent to the behavior because of the transference relationship and her emotional involvement with the therapist. It is the responsibility of the therapist not to let such behavior occur, because it is by definition an abuse of the transference relationship. Presumably, the therapist is properly trained in the mechanism of transference and uses it to the benefit of his patients rather than to the patient's detriment. When the patient expresses love to the therapist, this is usually out of transference and not as a reality of the relationship between the patient and the therapist as individuals. This is the patient responding to her own needs within the therapy situation. It is the responsibility—the obligation—of the therapist to deal with this transference phenomenon within the therapy and not to exploit it.

Nonprofessional Involvement

If the therapist falls in love with his patient, it is his responsibility to stop making medical or clinical decisions about his patient and to decide, with the patient, whether they wish to have a romantic relationship or a professional one. *The two may not coexist*. If they decide on the latter, the therapist should make every effort to find a suitable colleague to treat the patient. It is not appropriate to excuse nonprofessional behavior by separating the social hour from the therapy hour; and certainly it is not appropriate to charge money for sexual "therapy."

Seductiveness

With respect to the claim that it was the patient's seductiveness to which the therapist responded, this again betrays a mishandling of the transference and constitutes inappropriate behavior on the part of the therapist. In this type of situation the recommendation is for the therapist to stop treating patients altogether and to begin to seek treatment for himself. Some have determined that therapists of this type fall under the category of the "impaired physician," much as do the alcoholic and drug-addicted physician or other professional.

Therapeutic Sex

With respect to the claim by some therapists that they have sexual relations with their patients because it is therapeutic and helpful to the patient, one can only state that this is sheer nonsense. McCartney (1966) has written on the "overt transference," wherein he recommends such treatment with particular patients. Sheppard (1971) also has indicated that he and other colleagues of his have found sexual relations with patients to be helpful and therapeutic. Most therapists, however, maintain very clearly that sexual relations with patients are not therapeutic and, in fact, are detrimental and emotionally harmful. All ethics committees of all professional therapy organizations have proclaimed the prohibition against therapist–patient sexual interaction. All have debunked the notion that such behavior is therapeutic, and no responsible professional has ever accepted that version. It, too, is clearly a mishandling of the transference, and one certainly must question for whose benefit the sexual relationship is engendered.

Harmful Results

Newman (1979) has written on his extensive work with patients who have had sexual relations with former therapists and some of the difficulties they have had emotionally as a result of their former therapists' indiscretion and negligent acts. Others have experienced the reluctance of patients to become actively reinvolved in therapy once they have been betrayed. Several cases illustrate the difficulties for patients in these situations (*Landau* v. *Werner*, 1961; *Roy* v. *Hartogs*, 1975; *Zipkin* v. *Freeman*, 1968). Perhaps the most tragic case of all, which is not written up, is that involving a 25-year-old female nurse who was sexually involved with her psychiatrist, became pregnant, and wished to have an abortion. When she consulted her gynecologist, who knew that she was in treatment with the psychiatrist, her gynecologist felt it was appropriate to consult her therapist to determine whether she was "psychologically sound" enough to have the abortion. After the psychiatrist refused to give psychiatric clearance for the operation, the patient went to her psychiatrist's home, wrote a note implicating him in her current misery, and proceeded to kill herself on his property. The coroner's inquest determined that the psychiatrist was not directly responsible for her death and no criminal charges were pressed. The woman's father sued the psychiatrist for mishandling the transference and for inappropriate professional behavior resulting in the death of his daughter.

This inappropriate behavior has been viewed as incestuous by many observers. In an attempt to study this phenomenon, we did a survey (Sadoff & Showell, 1981) of 200 female psychiatrists in the United States to ascertain whether women psychiatrists become sexually involved with their patients in similar numbers as male psychiatrists. We used for comparison a previous study by Kardener, Fuller, & Mensh (1973), in which 5 percent of the psychiatrists surveyed (all of whom were male) admitted to having sexual relations with their patients. Our survey revealed that less than 1 percent of the respondents ($N = 101$) admitted to sexual relations with a patient; that is, one woman admitted to one isolated homosexual relationship with a patient. All the others indicated they utilized nonerotic touching but no sexual involvement. They utilized more appropriate means of dealing with sexual comments by their patients, and they admitted that they themselves at times, had sexual feelings toward their patients which they handled in appropriate ways without acting them out. None felt it would be therapeutic to have sexual intercourse with patients.

Summary

Thus we see that malpractice considerations may be related to inappropriate disclosures of information, treatment without infomed consent, negligence in suicidal or homicidal behavior by patients, and mishandling the transference in psychotherapy. Therapists should be aware of the duty they owe their patients and should treat their patients with diligence, according to the standards of care, in such a way as to avoid neglect of and injury to the patient.

In the event a mental health professional is sued in malpractice, it is most important that she contact her attorney and/or malpractice insurance representative. It is essential to follow the attorney's advice in these very complicated legal actions. The lawsuit may be emotionally traumatic, fatiguing, and financially draining on the clinician; thus, it is imperative—wherever possible—to avoid and prevent such lawsuits both by adhering to previously established guidelines and by working within acceptable community standards of care.

References

Cohen R. J. *Malpractice: A Guide for Mental Health Practitioners*, New York: Free Press, 1979.

Dawidoff, D. J. *The Malpractice of Psychiatrists*. Springfield, Ill.: Charles C Thomas, 1973.

Halleck, S. L. *Law in the Practice of Psychiatry: A Handbook for Clinicians*. New York: Plenum Medical Book Co., 1980.

Kardner, S. H., Fuller, M., & Mensh, I. N. A Survey of Physicians' Attitudes and Practices regarding Erotic and Non-Erotic Contact with Patients. *American Journal of Psychiatry*, *130*:10, October 1973, 1077–1081.

Landau v. Werner. 105 Sol. J. 257 (Q. B.), 1961.

McCartney, J. Overt Transference. *Journal of Sex Research, 2;* November 1966, 227–237.

Newman, R. Personal communication, June, 1979.

Roy v. Hartogs. 81 Misc. 2d 350, 366 N.Y.S. 2d 297 (Civ Ct. N.Y.), 1975.

Sadoff, R. L., & Showell, R. Sex and Therapy: A Survey of Female Psychiatrists. Presented at annual meeting, American Psychiatric Association, New Orleans, May 1981.

Sheppard, M. *The Love Treatment: Sexual Intimacy between Patients and Psychotherapists.* New York: Paperback Library, 1971.

Zipkin v. Freeman. 436 SW 2d, 753 (Mo.), 1968.

PART II

Traditional Legal Considerations in Mental Health Professions

Chapter ~

The Evaluation of Competency
in Psychiatric Patients

Determination of competency may be a very complicated matter, depending upon the person examined and the purpose for which competency is assessed. There are a number of areas in civil law, plus several in criminal law, where competency becomes a significant legal issue.

Competency in Criminal Proceedings

In criminal law, an expert may be called upon to evaluate a defendant to determine whether he is competent to stand trial, to plead, to be executed, to serve a sentence, and/or to give a confession. A witness in a criminal matter may be evaluated to determine his competence to testify in court.

Criminal law develops a number of criteria for each purpose for which competency is determined. For example, in order to be competent to stand trial, a defendant must know the nature and consequences of her legal situation and be able to confer with counsel in preparing a rational defense. Does that mean that she cannot have amnesia for the time of the crime? Must she know all the details about the legal and criminal process so that she can understand completely what is happening to her at every stage of development? Must she have a rational as well as a factual understanding of the charges and of her role within the procedure? Does that mean that, if a person requires psychotropic medication in order to be free of hallucinations and delusions, she is only "chemically competent" and without medication would not be competent? The answers vary in different jurisdictions. Thus, the complexity of determination of competency becomes more apparent.

Another feature that needs to be examined is the nature of the illness or condition of the person being evaluated. Is it a person's mental retardation that precludes him from knowing what he is doing, or is it the psychosis that distorts his perception such that he misinterprets the data around him? Perhaps his inability to understand is based on organic brain damage that may be due to trauma, infection, or toxic substances.

Generally, in determination of competency, the question becomes,

"Competency to do what?" or, "Competency for what purpose?" The law prescribes specific criteria for each purpose; the role of the examining psychiatrist and/or psychologist is to determine the nature of the person's illness or disability and how this interferes with his ability to know or understand certain issues or carry out particular functions.

Competency in Civil Proceedings

In civil law, the variety and complexity of examinations is even greater than for criminal law. People may be examined to determine their competency to enter into a contract, to get married, to write a will, to testify in court, to manage their own affairs, to decide upon their own medical treatment, to vote, to own property, or to engage in business. For each purpose, there are particular questions that generally assess the person's ability to understand the nature of the proceeding in which she is involved and her role within that proceeding.

A person may be competent for one purpose and incompetent for another. For example, an individual may be competent to write a will but not competent to manage her own affairs at that time. An example is the elderly woman, a nursing-home resident, who had been widowed and left the responsibility of caring for an estate. She had little or no idea about how much money there was, in what form it existed, or how to spend it on a daily basis. A relative of hers handled her affairs for her at the time, with her consent, so there was no need to declare her incompetent formally. At the same time, the woman knew generally how much money she had and to whom she wished to leave her estate. Thus, she was competent to write a will and to assign where her money would go after her death.

Competency for each separate purpose must be assessed independently. Psychiatrists often are called upon to give an opinion, but the final determination of competency belongs to the court. Courts are very careful not to deprive a person in any area of self-determination unless the court is convinced that the person declared incompetent is so severely ill and so disoriented with respect to time, place, or person that he is deprived of ability to know what he is about.

Competency to Participate
in Treatment

Determination of competency is most significant for the mental health practitioner in the area of a patient's decision-making ability in her own treatment. Currently, patients are being given increasing rights by the courts to determine the course of their treatment within the hospital or other treatment setting. Patients now are accorded the right to adequate treatment and, under certain circumstances, the right to refuse certain types of treatment or medication. It is essential for the treating physician to listen to the patient and also to allow the patient, to the extent possible, to participate in the decision making about her own treatment. The patient does not always know what is best for her, but very often has a good idea about what might not be good for her; thus, she has the right to complain and to resist certain forms of treatment that she believes may harm her. If the decision to refuse treatment is made out of delusion or of psychotic thought disorder, the physician may go ahead and treat if it is an emergency, or may wait to treat after a guardian is appointed if there is no emergency. A judge may declare a patient incompetent and order the physician to proceed with treatment as he sees best in the event of an urgent situation.

Let us take as examples the difficult situations that arose at the Boston State Hospital and in the state hospitals in New Jersey. In those states, the judges had declared in *Rogers* v. *Okin* (1979) and *Rennie* v. *Klein* (1979) that patients may refuse medication unless they are emergencies or unless they are incompetent to make the decision about their treatment. In the Rogers case, the court declared that the emergency had to be a significantly explosive one in which the patient was becoming imminently violent to himself or others, or had in fact become violent at the time. The judge in that case also declared that incompetency was to be determined only by the court. In the Rennie case, by contrast, Judge Brotman interpreted "emergency" to mean a significant change in the condition of the patient that could render him a significant danger of harm to self or others. He also allowed for "informal incompetency" to be determined by the treating physician in the event the patient was refusing medication because of his mental illness.

The physicians and nurses and others caring for the mentally ill patients require specific guidelines to help deal with patients who refuse medication or refuse treatment. They need to know whether they can treat a person against his will and under what circumstances and for how long a period of time. It is always wise to check with the hospital attorney if there are any questions about the competency of the patient or the nature of an emergency. It also is wise, when determining that an emergency exists, to have the input of a respected colleague, so the decision is not made idiosyncratically or un- ilaterally for the convenience of treating the patient against his will. It must be a bona fide emergency, documented by objective criteria, including, where possible, a second opinion.

In medicine generally, problems of competency arise when surgical patients refuse to have an operation or a life-saving procedure. The surgeon often becomes frustrated in her therapeutic efforts and turns to the psychia- trist for evaluation of her patient. She is looking for incompetency to decide about treatment, so that she may proceed with the operation and save her patient's life. Very often the patient will be found incompetent to make the decision, because of mental illness, senility, organic brain syndrome, or a combination of these. There are times, however, when a patient is merely frightened about disrupting the continuity of his body image and decides rationally and coherently that he does not wish to have the surgery and sustain the pain of recovery. Some choose to die, knowing that refusing the surgery will cause their death. This is not necessarily suicidal, nor is it a reflection of incompetency. Patients may decide rationally against life-saving surgery in order to avoid pain and to die with dignity. The concept of dying with dignity has been used increasingly in our society; hence, it is no longer believed generally that patients who refuse surgery of this type must be psychotic, confused, or incompetent.

One case comes to mind where an elderly woman was wheeled in to the office by her elderly husband, who had been caring for her for the year that had passed since she was told she must have an operation on her left foot to remove gangrene. She had continued to refuse the surgery, and the gangrene now was quite obvious. She was told that if she did not have the surgery she would die, and she chose not to have the surgery. She was referred for psychiatric evaluation by her surgeon because he believed she was incompetent to decide not to have surgery. On examination, the patient appeared to be a reasonably healthy woman in her mid-to-late 70s who sat in a wheelchair with her foot bandaged and wrapped in plastic. She related how she had it washed and cleaned and treated three times a day and how well cared for she was by her husband, whom she had cared for during his medical problems for the past 20 years. She was pleased with the attention she was receiving, and she also was aware that the line of gangrene had not ascended and that she was in no immediate danger. After discussing her situation for over an hour, she confided in the psychiatrist that "of course" she was not crazy and that if she found her foot getting worse she would have the surgery to avoid the fatal consequences of refusing it. However, she repeated that, since there was a discontinuation of the progress of the gangrene, she was in no immediate danger. She said very clearly that she would have the surgery when she decided the time was right. On that basis, she was found to be competent and she continued her conservative treatment for several more months until it became obvious that she required surgery as a life-saving measure. At that point she agreed, and the surgery was performed without undue side-effects.

Conflict in Assessing Competency

It is important for the clinician who is assessing competency to be aware of all the ramifications of the case she is evaluating. In one particular individual there may be more than one area to be assessed for competency. Recently, a mentally retarded woman was referred to a forensic psychiatrist because she claimed she had been raped at the institution for the mentally retarded by another individual who resided there. The question arose whether she would be competent to present testimony in court against the defendant in behalf of the prosecution. One psychiatrist examined her and gave the opinion that she was not competent to consent to sexual intercourse, and, therefore, the act constituted rape because it could not have been conducted with her consent. He also was of the opinion that she was mentally competent to provide testimony, even under cross-examination.

The matter was referred by the defense to another expert, who reached the opposite conclusion. He examined the witness and gave the opinion that she was incompetent to provide testimony since she had no basic understanding of what she would be doing in court or who would be present, and because she was not able to sit sufficiently still to stay in the witness stand without physical help from the attendants. She also was not able to keep her mind on the matter for sufficiently long periods of time to provide coherent responses. During the course of the examination, she also stated very clearly that she was angry at the person who offered her $2.00 for sexual intercourse because if she wanted to "go to bed with someone" she would do it with her boyfriend because she wanted to and "not because someone pays me to do it." On that basis the second clinican found her to be competent to give consent or withhold it, as she chose.

Here we have a classic example of the basic conflict between and among professionals about determination of competency. It is essential to provide the information and the data on which the conclusions are based, and not just to give conclusions about competency that meet the particular needs of the side that calls the expert for consultation.

It is important to put in a word here about the evaluation of individuals with the prospect of testifying in court. All too often, individuals who are sent to mental health professionals for evaluation for legal purposes are sent involuntarily and have no particular reason to be honest with the examiner or to be as open as they would if they came voluntarily as patients. When a person is hurting emotionally or physically, he seeks medical attention to relieve the pain. For that purpose, he is more likely to be honest and open about his symptoms than he would be if he were sent because someone else was concerned about his mental state. Therefore, it is especially important in conducting forensic psychiatric examinations for the examiner to provide, whenever possible, verbatim data as evidence on which to support her medical–legal conclusions. So it is with competency. The expert will need to be able to relate in court the particular questions that she asked the examinee and the responses that were given. Her interpretation of these responses then is open to cross-examination, which may be assessed by the judge.

Degree of Proof in Court

Obtaining medical and scientific data on which to base a medical, psychiatric, or psychological conclusion differs from obtaining evidence to be used in court to prove a matter within a particular level of certainty. In the law, there are three levels of proof:

    1. *The preponderance of the evidence*. This means that a judge or juror will assess the evidence and will believe it because it appears likely to have occurred in just over 50 percent of such instances, or there is a greater than 50 percent likelihood that the data are credible. This is the standard for civil cases.

    2. *Beyond a reasonable doubt*. This is the standard for criminal cases, which suggests about 90 percent or 95 percent certainty on the part of the jury with respect to their verdict.

    3. *Clear and convincing evidence*. Here is the middle ground, which implies about 70 percent to 75 percent certainty and is the standard for commitment of persons to hospitals under the *Addington* v. *Texas* (1979) rule. "Within reasonable medical certainty" also may approach the 70 percent or 75 percent mark of certainty, within the court's concept of "clear and convincing evidence"; however, no one has equated medical certainty with legal evidentiary certainty.

Testifying as an Expert Witness

Here we raise the question of the competency of the examiner, as well as the examinee. Who is competent to give in court an opinion about competency of a particular person? The court recognizes physicians as expert medical witnesses if they are licensed to practice medicine. They do not necessarily need to be licensed in that particular state. A general physician, however, should not expect to testify to the expertise that a psychiatrist, surgeon, or hematologist may testify to. The physician should stay within the limits of his expertise. For example, a psychiatrist who has little or no experience conducting or administering psychological tests should not begin to testify as an expert in psychology; and the psychiatric nurse should be able to testify to particular expertise in the care and treatment of psychiatric patients, which other nurses may not be able to do.

    The reason a person is accorded expertise in court is because she has particular training and/or experience in a field not available to the average, intelligent layperson. Expert testimony differs from factual testimony in that the expert may give opinions based upon her background and experience. This is a special privilege in court that is not accorded to factual witnesses.

There are particular rules of evidence involved in allowing persons to testify, either in a factual way or with opinions included. It is for this reason that anyone who testifies in court should be prepared properly, by the attorney calling her to testify, before she enters the courtroom. She should be fully aware of the complexities of the courtroom procedure and the issues at hand, including those that may be asked of her on cross-examination.

Essentially, the expert working in the field of law and psychiatry acts as a consultant to a particular side, since the courtroom situation is adversarial in nature; that is, involving the contesting of a particular question before an arbiter called the judge. The lawyers are engaged in a battle, each wishing to determine the rightness or justness of his particular argument. They present their cases in a logical, sequential manner, utilizing expert witnesses where possible. In many cases, psychiatrists, psychologists, social workers, psychiatric nurses, or others are called as experts to provide further clarification or interpretation of data. The expert should consider herself to be in the role of a teacher who is there to shed light on a particular situation in court and not to continue the development of the lawyer's argument. The lawyer is doing battle; the expert witness is not and must not get caught up in the adversary process. Rather, she offers a credible opinion that is supported by data to the extent possible. Scientific proof is often unavailable, but the testimony should not descend to the level of speculation. Basically, the testimony is reflective of the discipline of psychiatry and mental health practice.

Summary

Thus, competency in the law is assessed in individuals for particular purposes in both criminal and civil matters. Competency, however, is also relevant to the nature of the assessor, who professes to be competent both to make the examination and to provide adequate consultation and possible subsequent testimony for the attorney who engages him. Competency is a complicated issue and reflects the particular purpose in mind. The psychiatrist must be clearly aware of the nature of both the legal questions and the medical conditions he is evaluating. He must be able to relate medical problems to the legal questions, in order to assess properly a person's competency for a particular purpose.

References

Addington v. Texas. 441 U.S. 418, 1979.
Rennie v. Klein. 462 F. Supp. 1131 D.N.J., 1979.
Rogers v. Okin. 478 F. Supp. 1342 D. Mass., 1979.

Chapter 10

Personal Injury

Tort Actions

Perhaps one of the most important areas in forensic psychiatry is the field of personal injury. This area includes tort injuries, worker's compensation, and social security disability evaluations. Injuries due to tort include malpractice considerations and automobile accidents, as well as other injuries where fault is assessed. A tort is defined as a noncriminal wrong; therefore the area falls within civil law.

The expert may be called upon to evaluate an individual who has been injured in an accident where someone will be blamed for negligence. This accident may be on the highways, in the air, on the railroad, at work, at home, or in the doctor's office.

Worker's compensation differs from tort action in that an agreement was made to provide the injured party with immediate payments for time lost at work and for medical expenses in exchange for his not filing a lawsuit against his employer. This compromise helps both parties in that it allows the patient to receive immediate medical treatment without expense and to have living expenses paid through a partial salary for the time that he is disabled. It helps the employer because the person injured at work is then precluded from filing a lawsuit against his employer for negligence; however, the employee who is injured is not precluded from filing a lawsuit for negligence against the manufacturer of the equipment that may have been faulty when used at the place of employment.

Social Security Disability Evaluations

Examination for social security disability or insurance disability is a different evaluation, which includes no area of fault and where it is not necessary to equate the person's illness with an injury. It is sufficient for the expert to indicate that the examinee has a significant mental illness that renders him disabled or partially disabled from working. There are particular criteria that are spelled out by the Social Security Agency defining disability and percentages of disability.

Assessment of Injury and Etiology of Symptoms

Responsibilities of the Expert Consultant

In the assessment of patients in personal-injury matters, clinicians must stay within their area of expertise and not traverse into the surgical or medical area. For example, if they are asked to examine a patient who has been injured following faulty surgery, they should not presume to comment on the correctness or incorrectness of the surgical procedure, but confine their evaluation to their area of expertise in psychiatry. That is, clinicians should evaluate such patients for depression or anxiety or mental illness that may have resulted from, or been caused by, or aggravated by, the surgery. Whether or not the surgery was done correctly would be a matter for the jury or the court to decide after hearing the expert testimony of another surgeon.

Similarly, experts may not comment on the liability of particular parties in accidents, but may comment on the person's state of mind, which may have contributed to negligence or lack of it. Thus, if the person examined had been drinking heavily prior to his automobile accident, that factor is relevant. If the examinee has a history of seizures that was not previously disclosed and then was injured at work from a fall, hitting his head on heavy machinery and causing a concussion, it is relevant to know that he had seizures prior to the head injury. His fall may have resulted from his seizure.

Importance of Complete History

The field of personal injury for the mental health professional has been a confusing one, with a myriad of labels given to the psychiatric conditions that follow trauma. Such labels as traumatic neurosis, compensation neurosis, shell shock, traumatic amnesia, postaccident anxiety syndrome, posttraumatic psychosis, and malingering have all been utilized in this area. Robitscher, in his book, *Psychiatry and Law: Pursuit of Agreement* (1966), clarifies the issue when he provides three categories to explain a person's symptoms following an injury:

1. *Traumatic neurosis*. A healthy individual became mentally ill as the result of an overwhelming stress.

2. *Compensation or triggered neurosis.* The individual had a latent illness triggered or precipitated by the trauma and held on to by the patient for largely unconscious reasons.
3. *Malingering.* The individual consciously deceives. [p. 107]

It becomes extremely important for the examiner to take a careful and accurate history of the patient's condition prior to her injury. In addition to the history, which must be supplemented by interviews with other people who know the patient and by records from school, work, other hospitals, and physicians, the injured person must be carefully examined by the psychiatrist and also be given a complete medical, neurological examination. It is particularly relevant in the area of personal injury that psychiatrists have a medical background to be able accurately to assess these conditions and to be able to read and understand the medical reports of other physicians and hospitals. Integrating psychological, psychiatric, and medical findings is an essential ingredient in preparing forensic psychiatric opinions for the courts, which require evidence beyond the verbal presentations of the patient. The careful examination is necessary but not sufficient. Records and other data will be needed to confirm or deny clinical impressions and preliminary diagnoses.

Two examples of such thorough interviews come to mind. In the first case, a 23-year-old woman was referred for forensic psychiatric examination one year after she was hit over the head with a wooden chair in a barroom fight. She had been depressed for several months, and her attorney believed her depression was related directly to the concussion she sustained in the fight one year previously. The examiner also interviewed the patient's brother and father as part of his comprehensive examination. There was no question the woman was depressed and had been depressed for several months. It remained to determine the origin of the depression. Was it due to the blow on the head and the fight she had had, or was it due to other contemporaneous causes? Careful questioning revealed that the woman's mother had suffered a heart attack six months previously, and was requiring the woman to remain at home to take care of three younger siblings. This resulted in her dropping out of school, losing her boyfriend, and being homebound for several months. It seemed more reasonable to assume that the latter set of events was related more directly to her depression than a blow to the head one year before. In this case, the forensic psychiatrist helped the plaintiff's attorney by recommending dropping the claim for mental or emotional damages, since it would be impossible to prove and unlikely to be believed.

A second case involved multiple traumata to a person, including three automobile accidents within one year. The case in point involved the middle accident. It was virtually impossible to prove that that particular accident caused the emotional anxiety and phobia of driving when the patient had been involved in two other accidents, the first occurring one month before and the last happening two months subsequent to the one in question. It was most likely that the combination of all three accidents within a short period of time had led to the severity of anxiety and phobic symptoms relevant to driving. It would be spurious thinking to focus the anxiety and phobia on a specific accident, excluding the others primarily because an attorney was more interested in a particular accident than the other two.

Examiner Objectivity

Both of these cases illustrate not only the questionable nature of etiology or causation of emotional symptoms from trauma and the need for careful history, but also point out the potential for deception within this whole field of personal injury and mental illness. Because the plaintiff may deceive or simulate mental illness or blame it on a particular injury in order to be compensated, it is especially important for examiners to maintain a high degree of credibility and integrity in their examinations. They must not be influenced unduly by the plaintiff's attorney to find a cause and effect when none exists or when the etiology is in question. In fact, examiners can do more harm to attorneys' cases by giving them what they want rather than what they need. What they need is a careful and accurate assessment of the total picture, in order to know what they are dealing with and in order to enter the case fully confident that their positions are sound, not only legally, but also from a mental health standpoint. If attorneys are given opinions that fit their cases but are not based on sound clinical principles, then they are likely to be disappointed in the end. In addition, the consultant's credibility will be damaged.

Use of Hospital Records

As in all cases in forensic mental health, hospital and physician records are extremely important in determining the degree of illness and its etiology. In personal-injury cases, nursing notes are particularly of value for later assessment. When a person is hospitalized following an injury, it is important for careful records to be developed within the hospital as well as within the doctor's office. These records later may form the basis of argument regarding the patient's illness. It is only fair to the patient that he be compensated properly for his illness if that is the just and proper direction. To deprive the patient of information and evidence that can be used to aid his case would not be appropriate. Thus, it is important to recognize the value of careful record keeping, especially in personal-injury cases. This is even more true in potential malpractice cases where the injury occurs within the hospital rather than before the patient is admitted to the hospital.

Hospital nurses are particularly astute in observing the behavior and comments of patients under their care. It is important to record behavior, attitudes, and comments (especially on psychiatric wards, but also on medical wards) of patients who are admitted for treatment of medical conditions following an injury. Attorneys find nursing notes to be most valuable, because they are spontaneous and are written without undue censorship or special caution. They also usually are more legible and easily read than some physicians' notes.

Occasionally, the expert is referred a case in which the patient had committed suicide while in the hospital. The patient may have jumped from a window that perhaps should not have been opened or may have hanged herself with her bathrobe ties which she perhaps should not have been given. Comments about suicidal potential, or spontaneous comments made by the patient about killing herself, or notes of her depression or her hopelessness are all extremely important and valid in assessing the patient's potential for suicidal behavior and the recommended treatment. Sometimes a patient may fall out of a window that was left open, not in a direct suicidal gesture, but as a result of confusion, disorientation, and distorted perception. Such comments in the notes regarding the patient's stability, orientation, and perception are all valid and necessary for proper determination of her state of mind at the time of her injury or death. Comments about visitors who upset the patient or who please her are also important. Notes of other therapists—such as physical, occupational, art, and library therapists, or nursing aides who spend a good deal of time with the patient—will be scrutinized in the event of a personal injury, either within the hospital or prior to admission.

The "Rule-Out" Syndrome

Another important consideration for the examiner in personal-injury cases is to be wary of the "rule-out" syndrome. In this instance, the patient is referred for consultation because, for example, he has not responded to physical treatment following an injury to his back or neck and the orthopedic surgeon, neurosurgeon, neurologist, or internist believes the patient may have "supratentorial" origin to his symptoms. The doctor therefore recommends a psychiatric examination, since her belief is that the symptoms are not based on organic etiology but rather on psychological conflict or conversion hysteria. It is essential for the consultant to make his own determination, based on his experience in the field and his knowledge of what psychological conflicts may lead to physical symptoms. He should not be content to find symptoms to be psychologically oriented just because other physicians have not found a physical etiology to the symptoms. It is possible that there may be an organic etiology that was not determined, or it may be possible that the patient is malingering or feigning illness. In two such cases, for example, patients were referred because no organic etiology was determined. In neither case were there found any clear-cut psychological conflicts that could explain the symptomatology. The recommendation by the examining forensic psychiatrist was to have a second medical opinion. In each case, a deeper study was conducted, organic pathology was determined, the patient had an operation for the condition, and on follow-up two years later was free of symptoms.

Testing

A careful forensic psychiatric examination may include psychological tests, neurological examination, further neurological testing, neuropsychological testing, further medical testing, and X-rays, before a final diagnosis of psychological etiology is made. This, of course, is not true in every case, but the possibility of nonpsychiatric origin of symptoms should be considered in every psychiatric examination and appropriate consultation should be obtained.

Perhaps the most common form of traumatic psychological illness is the postaccident anxiety syndrome, as described by Modlin (1967) of the Menninger Clinic. He lists the following symptoms, which should be evaluated in every patient complaining of disability or illness due to an accident or trauma:

1. Anxiety
2. Muscular tension
3. Irritability
4. Impaired concentration and memory
5. Repetitive nightmares
6. Sexual inhibition
7. Social withdrawal

Many of the symptoms are subjective and can be feigned by the patient; however, repetitive nightmares are an important feature if they are present. The nightmares are most common shortly after the accident and begin to taper off after about a year. If a person continues to have regular daily nightmares two years after the accident, the examiner should suspect malingering or exaggerating. Also the usual postaccident anxiety syndrome will begin to improve within a few months and be fairly short lived, running its course between 12 and 18 months. If a person continues to have symptoms two years or longer after the accident, the examiner should begin to think in terms of other injuries or other reasons for the symptoms. In addition to malingering, the examiner should be thinking of conversion hysteria, somatization of emotional conflicts, and, certainly, the secondary gain of disability.

Psychological testing is quite helpful in delineating the difference among traumatic neuroses, hysterical conversion symptoms, and the psychosomatic illnesses. Psychodynamics found on testing are important in the overall assessment of the person's condition. Most likely, the person with conversion hysteria or dissociation will show evidence for denial, repression, early hysterical personality features, and a pattern of handling stress by repression or suppression. The person with psychosomatic illness most often will have a history or pattern of somatizing in other areas, or of prolonged healing from operations or other illnesses. The person with secondary gain also will show a lengthy recovery period in his past history. Presence of organic brain damage following a concussion may not be detected by electroencephalogram, CAT scan, or neurological testing, but may be found on subtle neuropsychological testing, including the Reittan or Luria batteries.

Malingering or conscious deception may be detected by the presence of extreme symptoms that do not fit usual patterns of psychodynamics and appear to be exaggerated. Evidence may come from private investigators, who can detect gaps in a person's simulation of illness and record them on photographs, movies, or tape-recording devices.

In the field of personal injury, then, the forensic psychiatrist must be able

1. To work closely with psychologists, physicians of all specialties, lawyers, employers, family members, friends, and acquaintances
2. To take a comprehensive history and conduct a thorough examination before (a) concluding that a particular a set of symptoms constitute a bona fide medical or psychiatric syndrome and before (b) concluding within reasonable medical certainty that that syndrome is related to, and caused by, the injury sustained (Keiser, 1968).

Emotional Damage

It is one thing for a mental health expert to categorize a set of symptoms into a syndrome of mental illness as delineated in *DSM-III*. It is another for him to be able to state, within reasonable medical or scientific certainty, that that syndrome was caused by a specific trauma at a particular time. In order for him to do that accurately, he must know

1. What the person was like prior to that trauma
2. The extent of the trauma on his particular personality
3. The pattern that person has in reacting to stress of that type.

Later, he will be asked if there is a direct correlation between the injury and the syndrome, and what effect that syndrome has on the person's ability to function.

A forensic expert may find that, following an accident, a patient had sustained a degree of depression, anxiety, or even a specific phobic symptom. By the time the case comes to trial however, sometimes four or five years after the accident, the clinician will be in a position to reexamine the patient and may determine that the syndrome has either remitted, been partially or significantly resolved, or, if it continues to be present, does not affect significantly the person's ability to function. That is, the expert may be asked what degree or percentage of disability the patient continues to have as a result of his psychological or psychiatric illness. This is relevant in social security disability determinations and workers' compensation cases, as well as in tort actions. Here the expert not only must be in a position to define and describe the syndrome and to be able to relate it to a particular accident or injury, but she also must be able to state how that psychiatric illness keeps the patient from functioning in his personal, family, vocational, and/or social life.

The law would be particularly interested in the patient's professional or vocational pursuits, that is, whether the person is able to perform with the same degree of skill as he did before. If someone suffers a physical injury, such as an eye or hand injury, it would be more significant if that person were a surgeon than a psychiatrist. The psychiatrist presumably could continue to function as effectively even with an injured eye or hand, but a surgeon could not; hence, the law requests percentage of disability. In the area of emotional disability, however, this is a very difficult matter. In psychiatry or psychology, it is much more complicated to assess the degree of disability because a particular emotional reaction cannot easily be related *quantitatively* to a resulting inability to function. This is, however, the task of the mental health consultant, who, it is hoped, will be able to testify that a particular injury has affected a person's ability to function, sometimes either in total (so that he has complete disability) or not at all (such that he has no disability). She also may be able to state that a person has a partial disability and would be able to function at particular jobs but not at others, based on her knowledge and understanding of the work entailed on a particular job.

For example, if the injured person is a police officer, the expert may not be able to testify about the patient's ability to work unless she knows what the patient does on his job. One issue that continuously arises with injured police officers is whether they can function effectively and carry a gun. If there is significant depression or anger following an injury, the police officer may be precluded from carrying a gun to protect his own life and also to protect the safety of others. This partial disability may be temporary or be permanent, depending on the degree of recovery of the patient and the results of repeated examinations over time.

Treatment of the injured individual may become a long-term, difficult matter, fraught with great resistance and frequent explosions. A patient may become so angry at the people who caused her accident and injury, or at the people who are responsible for providing her with medical treatment, that she is unable to rehabilitate effectively until that anger and bitterness are resolved. Sometimes, the insurance company may believe the patient is faking and will not be cooperative in providing support for her treatment. In some cases, this lack of cooperation does hinder the treatment because the patient realizes that the insurance company thinks she is lying and shows no trust in her. She becomes increasingly angry, especially if there is a physical deformity that requires therapy. This is added to her emotional response to the accident and the deformity.

It should be noted that the law will consider emotional damage to individuals who observe or witness others being injured, even though they themselves are not so physically injured. For example, if a mother watches her youngster being hit by a car or killed in an accident, she is considered to be in the "zone of danger," and she may be compensated for the pain, suffering, and mental illness that ensues from that accident. Lack of consortium also may be compensated for if a patient is injured such that he or she cannot perform properly within the marriage. The surviving spouse, or the uninjured spouse, may be compensated for the lack of consortium or marital gratification of which she or he was deprived as a result of the accident.

Finally, a person may become psychotic as a result of an injury (Sadoff, 1973) and require long-term psychiatric hospitalization, including electroshock treatment and medication, that would not have been necessary without the injury. One case is that of a 34-year-old woman who slipped on the ice in a parking lot of a large department store, fell, and broke her leg. A few days later she was committed to the state hospital where she stayed for one year for treatment. She claimed in her suit for damages that her paranoid schizophrenic reaction, which required her hospitalization, resulted from the injury. This seemed unusual, and the insurance company questioned the validity of such a claim. On careful examination, however, the patient related that she was ruminating about her broken leg and believed that she would sustain a second broken leg and be crippled for life. This caused her great depression and inability to function, and she became significantly psychotic, requiring hospitalization. Past history revealed that she had been subject to a gall bladder operation five years previously. Following the surgery she also ruminated to the point that she believed she was going to die from the surgery and therefore could not function. She was admitted to the same state hospital where she stayed for six months for active treatment of her paranoid schizophrenic reaction. Because of the precedent, in a nonlitiginous matter, of the relationship between her psychotic illness following innocuous surgery, it was determined that this was a woman who reacted to physical stress in a particular manner, becoming psychotic, and her claim was allowed. Other cases of psychosis following trauma have been claimed, but they have been rejected, since traumatic psychosis is a rare entity and such a clear relationship as just described can not always be developed.

Summary

Traumatic illness is a clear-cut entity that requires careful assessment, comprehensive evaluation, and good record keeping. The cooperative efforts of physicians, psychiatrists, psychiatric nurses, psychologists, insurance companies, lawyers, and rehabilitation specialists are required for proper evaluation and management of people who sustain personal injuries and who require treatment for disability purposes.

References

Keiser, L. *The Traumatic Neurosis*. Philadelphia: Lippincott, 1968.

Modlin, H. C. The Post Accident Anxiety Syndrome: Psychosocial Aspects. *American Journal of Psychiatry, 123*:8, February 1967, 1008–1012.

Robitscher, J. Mental Suffering and Traumatic Neurosis, Chapter 12 in *Psychiatry and the Law: Pursuit of Agreement*. Philadelphia: Lippincott, 1966.

Sadoff, R. L. Traumatic Psychosis. In L. R. Frumer & M. K. Minzer (Eds.), *Personal Injury Annual*. New York: Matthew Bender, 1973.

Chapter 11

Domestic Relations

Domestic relations law, which operates in the areas of marriage, divorce, annulment, child custody, visitation, and child abuse, is an important area of forensic psychiatry. The forensic expert must be aware not only of the legal implications involved in proceedings such as divorce and custody matters, but also of family psychodynamics and developmental aspects in psychiatry and psychology. Preferably, a child psychiatrist or psychologist should be consulted if the children involved in the dispute are under the age of eight years. The emergence of child forensic psychiatry is clearly reflective of the need for child psychiatrists in the area of domestic relations matters.

Marital Status

Marriage

Taking each issue individually in this area, we begin with marriage. People getting married must be competent to enter into the contract of marriage; that is, they must know the nature and consequences of their agreement to marry another. There have been challenges to marriages on the basis of age differential, mental retardation, and psychotic illness. If one partner is deemed to be exploitative of another and encourages marriage through fraud or willful design over a weakened intellect, the validity of the marriage may be challenged. A marriage contract is said to be void if it was made inappropriately or was illegal in the first place. Thus, if a person who is already married marries another, the second marriage is null and void. If, however, a person marries a mentally retarded individual who does not understand the consequences of marriage, the marriage may be voidable by court order after an appropriate hearing on the issues.

Annulment

Annulments are not granted as freely as previously, in order to protect the welfare of the offspring. Since divorce has become relatively easier in most jurisdictions, the option is for divorce rather than annulment. An annulment implies there was no valid marriage in the first place, so the children of the marriage would be considered illegitimate unless the law protected their legitimacy.

Divorce

In divorce proceedings, the older ruling of "fault" (rather than the newer "no-fault" concept) requires that there must be an injured and innocent spouse as well as one who is blameworthy for the breakup of the marriage. If both partners admit to adulterous or other irresponsible behavior that could destroy the marriage, the law may maintain the integrity of the marriage, since both partners would have been at fault and there would not be one innocent and injured spouse. Also, collusion is not valid for divorce under the older method. People cannot agree to get divorced. It must be a contest in which one person finds fault with the behavior of the other spouse.

Under the older ruling, mental illness may be both a factor in divorce and also a defense against it. If a person is so mentally ill that he cannot form the specific intent to commit the indignities of which he is charged, then the divorce may not be granted, since the offending spouse would have a valid defense against the offensive behavior. If, however, the mentally ill spouse is so severely mentally ill that it is unlikely that he will recover in a reasonable or a foreseeable time, usually three years, and has required hospitalization for that period of time, the nonmedically ill spouse may obtain a divorce on the grounds of incurable insanity or incurable mental illness. Thus, the forensic mental health expert may be called to evaluate individuals seeking divorce or seeking to prevent divorce depending on the nature of the mental illness, its extent, and prognosis.

Child-Custody and -Visitation Proceedings

General Custody Proceedings

By far the most important areas of domestic relations law for mental health professionals occur in the child-custody and -visitation areas. Once the parties have agreed upon a divorce, where there are children available for a custody battle, the problems usually begin. The children are innocent victims of such battles and do not fare well when the parents choose to exploit them in the battles the parents have with each other.

In the past, the courts adhered to the "tender years" doctrine, whereby the children were given to the mother's care unless it could be proven that she was an unfit mother. Usually that meant she was immoral, or was living with different men, or bringing a number of "uncles" into the household. This was deemed a matter of moral turpitude that would not be tolerated by the court in the raising of children. If it could be shown that the mother was unfit, the children would go almost automatically to the father, without much evaluation of his moral code. In those days, the double standard of morality adhered, and fathers could get away with behavior that would not be tolerated in mothers.

Currently, the concept rests on the "best interest of the child," rather than on the tender years doctrine. Each parent has an equal opportunity to present his or her case to obtain custody of the child or children. The court then must decide which parent would have the best opportunity to raise the children in the most favorable manner for the children. This would be determined by testimony of witnesses, including psychiatrists, psychologists, social workers, and others. In this instance, it may be necessary for the examiner to make a home visit to determine the structure of the environment to which the child might be sent. Courts have stated specifically that the amount of money available is not a factor in determining best interest; rather, courts seek the atmosphere and environment that would be most conducive to appropriate growth and development of the children. Occasionally, the court may find that neither parent can present an effective or adequate environment for the child, so the court may order the children to be placed in a foster home or a public welfare agency until reasonable accommodations can be found.

Sometimes the battle is not between the parents, but between one parent and the youth and family services agency of a particular county or state. Here, the parent would be accused of child abuse or neglect, and the agency would be attempting to prove to the judge that the children would not be well off at home with both parents or with either parent, because they are being physically beaten or emotionally abused and neglected. Evidence here can come from neighbors, school teachers, friends, and relatives. The court places great emphasis on the emotional well-being of children and therefore will seek appropriate psychiatric and psychological consultation in order to arrive at a reasonable decision consistent with current medical and psychiatric theories.

In conducting the examination, it is best for the forensic examiner to have access to all parties involved, preferably at the request of the court. Because this is an adversary proceeding, the psychiatrist may have access only to the party who calls him and approves of his presence in the case. The other side might refuse his examination for valid reasons and call in its own expert.

In making the examination, the expert has the opportunity of evaluating both the relationship between one parent and the children and the mental health of all the children. Comparative statements should not be made where only one side has been examined. There is often distortion in cases of this type, and the psychiatrist should not let himself be manipulated or become caught in the middle of the battle between and among the family members.

Certainly the children should be consulted if they are old enough to be verbal and to have a mature view of the situation. Most children do have a preference but may be too frightened to express it, because of their concern about alienating the other parent. Those children who are excessively anxious about testifying in court should be allowed to testify to the judge in chambers if they choose, or should not be forced to make a preference if they choose not to. Some adolescents, however, do wish to be heard and often are concerned when they are not consulted and their wishes are ignored by the court. For best results, the court should explain to the children its reasons, if it rejects the child's wishes in favor of what the court sees as the child's needs.

Psychosis and Parental Competency

Psychosis alone is not sufficient grounds to preclude custody. In one case, a 42-year-old paranoid schizophrenic man, who was seeing a psychotherapist, was caring for his four sons, who had been abandoned by their mother. The people from the welfare agency learned of his bizarre behavior at home and petitioned to have the court find a new home for the children. The boys ranged in age from 9 to 13 and wished to remain with their father. Upon examination, it was clear that the father was actively psychotic, but he confined his delusional system to his belief that he was a Buddhist monk. At home he would practice his religious rituals by himself and would not impose them on the children. By contrast, he was quite responsible in having them clothed and fed properly and in seeing that they attended medical examinations and school functions regularly and with discipline. The boys acknowledged that their father was "weird" but did not impose his bizarre behavior on them. The court allowed the father to keep the children but recommended that he continue with his psychotherapy.

Homosexuality and Parental Competency

Homosexuality, in and of itself, also does not preclude a parent from caring for her or his child. In a case that was referred to the Forensic Psychiatry Clinic at the University of Pennsylvania, a 33-year-old lesbian mother was accused by her mother, the grandmother of her 9-year-old daughter, of not being a good mother. The grandmother petitioned for the right to raise the child and take her from her mother. On evaluation, it was clear that the mother was, in fact, a lesbian and did have active sexual relations with one particular woman, who visited the home twice weekly as Aunt Judy. There was a good relationship between Judy and the youngster, who did not suspect a homosexual involvement with her mother. The grandmother dropped the petition when she was told that it would be difficult for her to pursue her claim if her argument was that she was worried that her daughter would raise her granddaughter to be a lesbian, because, if that worry were considered by the court to be legitimate (which it is not), then the court would be loath to give the grandmother a second chance at raising another lesbian.

Other Areas of Competency

What the court is most concerned about is violent, bizarre sexual behavior; criminal behavior; or moral turpitude. One woman was not able to keep her daughter because she had been arrested and convicted for forgery. The court took the child away, upon petition of the father as a result of the mother's conviction. After the mother served her sentence and returned to a normal state of rehabilitation, the court was convinced that this was a one-time episode and not a pattern of criminal or antisocial behavior that would affect her youngster adversely. The daughter was returned to her following a proper hearing.

Visitation Proceedings

Visitation may impose an even more difficult problem than custody, since flexibility here is the key. Some have acknowledged that joint custody would be preferable to the kind of weekend visitation that serves only to alienate parents and negatively affect the child. If the parents get along with each other reasonably well and live near each other, joint custody has been recommended as the more appropriate solution. However, that condition is so rare that, if it is not feasible, then custody usually is awarded to one parent and visitation privileges to the other.

The fact of having custody of the child gives power to the custodial parent over the visiting parent. The visiting parent does have some power in the arrangement and may use it by not coming to visit when it is time, or by trying to come more frequently than is allowed, or by spending more time than allowed.

If there is no manipulation in the relationship between the parents, then the flexibility that is consistent with the best wishes and needs of the children should be the goal. Rigidity without rationality is to be avoided, except that a disciplined structure of visitation for younger children may be more conducive to healthy development than an erratic, unpredictable schedule of visitation.

Sometimes a mother will not allow the father to visit if he is behind in his child-support payments. This attitude, again, only serves to alienate the children and is not conducive to healthy growth and development.

What is needed in such cases is divorce counseling or visitation counseling, which may be imposed by the court when it makes a decision about custody and visitation. Counseling is necessary in many cases in order to avoid the kind of built-in difficulties that only can affect the children negatively. The children do much better if they can see both parents at relatively frequent intervals and in an nontraumatic way. Sometimes, if the visitation is excessively traumatic and leads to psychophysiological responses (enuresis, rashes, gastrointestinal disorders, vomiting), behavioral difficulties, or night terrors on the part of the children, the visitation may be curtailed temporarily until help is obtained for the child.

Courts do not like to split the children between the parents, but sometimes they will do so if it can be shown that this will be in the best interests of the children. Occasionally, the daughter will go with the mother and the son with his father, if the relationship between the siblings is not strong but the attachment to the same-sex parent is favorable and necessary.

Sometimes the visitation and custody arrangements will have to be reviewed on a regular basis to determine whether they are meeting the needs of the children successfully. The judge may be told by the mental health experts that the arrangements should be for the next year or six months, at which time a review of the environment and situation should be made by the mental health team to note progress or difficulty in meeting the children's needs. Mostly, however, the children do better if the arrangements are seen as permanent for them, rather than temporary. The anxiety engendered in children by their not knowing whether they will live with their mother or father may be difficult to bear and impede their growth and development.

Whereas the involvement of forensic experts in domestic relations may be fraught with great difficulties, it poses an even greater challenge not only for current emotional problems but for preventive mental health in the children, who later may develop a pattern similar to their parents', especially if they divorce and have children in need of custodial assignment, or if they become abusing parents after having been abused children. The fact that the abused child often goes on to become an abusing parent is appropriate in this context. It is important to give the abused child, as well as the abusing parent, the kind of treatment that is necessary to prevent this progression into the next generation. Sexual abuse of daughters by their fathers is certainly more common than of sons by their mothers. The usual procedure of removing the father from the house during the period of treatment is important to help the daughter recover normally. However, there comes a time when there must be a reuniting, if the father has obtained treatment and made appropriate changes. Without a reconfrontation between daughter and father after proper treatment, there may develop lifelong patterns of neurotic or characterlogical difficulties.

Summary

Thus, the involvement of forensic psychiatrists in domestic relations law lies not only in the assessments necessary for court action but also in the evaluations of those in need of treatment. The challenge is significant and the training of child psychiatrists and psychologists in this area of forensic work is increasingly necessary. The reader interested in further illumination on this subject is referred to Goldstein, Freud, & Solnit (1973); Sadoff & Billick, 1981; and Schetky & Benedek (1980).

References

Goldstein, J., Freud, A., & Solnit, A. J. *Beyond the Best Interests of the Child*. New York: Free Press, 1973.
Sadoff, R. L., & Billick, S. The Legal Rights and Difficulties of Children in Separation and Divorce. In I. R. Stuart and L. E. Abt (Eds.), *Children of Separation and Divorce: Management and Treatment*. New York: Van Nostrand Reinhold, 1981.
Schetky, D. H., & Benedek, E. P. *Child Psychiatry and the Law*. New York: Brunner/Mazel, 1980.

Chapter 12

Criminal Law

History of Criminal Responsibility

Traditionally, mental health professionals have been called upon in criminal matters to evaluate defendants for competency and criminal responsibility. These two basic concepts have been expanded within the criminal law to include competency, not only to stand trial, but competency of the defendant at any stage in the legal proceedings. This includes her competency to give a statement or confession when first confronted by police before having her Miranda rights and warnings given, or following her formal accusation and arrest; competency to plead at any stage of the proceedings (for example, competency to plead guilty, to waive other rights, to testify in her own behalf, to be sentenced, or to be executed). (See Chapter 9, on Competency, for further delineation and explanation of this consideration.)

With respect to criminal responsibility, the issues have become complicated by the changes in the mental health acts in various jurisdictions. Traditionally, the M'Naughten Rule was invoked to determine whether a person had sufficient mental capacity at the time of the committing of a crime to know what he was doing and to know that it was wrong. Variations of this "right–wrong" test of criminal responsibility have been developed over the past 150 years, sometimes modifying M'Naughten and sometimes utilizing an entirely different concept.

A brief history of the laws on criminal responsibility reveals that the concept dates back to the thirteenth century, when Bracton, a Roman cleric and judge, determined that a defendant would have no criminal responsibility if he possessed mentation no more than a "wild brute" (Whitlock, 1963). The concept here was an all-or-none principle of understanding of one's position in life. If the defendant had no understanding and no rational thought processes, then he would not be found responsible for his behavior. If, however, he had any, he would be presumed to have sufficient for a finding of guilt. This extreme position was modified by Coke & Hale in the sixteenth century (Whitlock, 1963) when they developed divisions of mental illness for people who were found *non compos mentis* within specific categories.

The matter was refined by Thomas Erskine, who argued the case of

Hadfield in 1800 (Whitlock, 1963). Erskine brilliantly demonstrated the fallacy of the argument of the extreme position of the earlier legal commentators. He showed that a defendant may have some understanding and still not be responsible because of the delusions caused by his mental illness. The Hadfield case was especially significant because Hadfield had had brain damage from a war wound, which affected his judgment and his ability to reason. Erskine convinced the court that Hadfield should not be found criminally responsible, because his behavior was based primarily on his delusional system, which was caused by his brain damage and resulting mental illness.

The Hadfield delusion test remained in effect from 1800 through 1843, when Daniel M'Naughten was tried in Scotland for shooting the secretary of the Prime Minister of England (M'Naughten, 1843). M'Naughten was found not guilty by reason of insanity on the basis of the delusion test and was sent to Bethlehem or "Bedlam" at the Queen's pleasure. Queen Victoria, however, was quite disturbed at the number of defendants who had attacked her royal party or administrative officers and had been found not guilty by reason of insanity under the Hadfield delusion test. Therefore, she convinced the parliament to change the law from the delusion test to the so-called M'Naughten Rules of insanity. The judges, at the request of the House of Lords, clarified their thinking on standards of criminal responsibility and emerged with the well-known M'Naughten Test, which states that a person is not to be held criminally responsible for his behavior if it can be proved clearly that at the time of the committing of the act in question he was laboring under such a defect of reason, from disease of the mind, that he did not know the nature and quality of the act he was doing, or if he did know it, that he did not know that what he was doing was wrong. This is the statement of the so-called "right–wrong" test, which is a specific test for a person's particular state of mind, at a specific time, with reference to a particular act. It is for this reason that all "insanity" is "temporary."

Sometimes attorneys will disparage the notion of temporary insanity by alluding to its convenience at the time of the act. In truth, all insanity must be determined only for the time of the act and not for any other period of time. A defendant's mental illness may transcend her criminal act such that it extends beyond, or preceded, the act itself. However, the concept of insanity is one that has to do only with a particular point in time.

The M'Naughten Test is currently in existence in most of the states in the United States and in some other countries. It is basically a conservative test and relies primarily upon cognition. A person must "know," or have an intellectual awareness of, his act and its consequences and be aware that it is against the law. Wrongfulness usually refers to illegality rather than immorality.

Modifications of the M'Naughten Test include the addition of the "irresistible impulse" clause in the late nineteenth century (*Davis* v. *United States,* 1897). Irresistible impulse is involved currently in the insanity rules of 20 states and always follows the M'Naughten Rules; it never stands alone. The irresistible impulse modification to M'Naughten states that, if a person at the time of the crime did know the nature and quality of her act and did know that what she was doing was wrong, but still had a mental illness that affected her such that she could not resist committing the act, then she may be found to be not responsible. The issue here is irresistible impulse and not unresisted impulse. It must be shown that if a policeman were at the defendant's elbow, she still would have committed the act.

In 1869 and 1871, the State of New Hampshire, in the cases of *State* v. *Pike* and *State* v. *Jones,* respectively, changed the insanity rules to the antecedent of the now-defunct Durham decision of Washington, D.C. (*U.S.* v. *Durham,* 1954). The New Hampshire test states that a person would not be held responsible if her criminal behavior was an "offspring" of her mental illness. (This is always a jury question; as a result, the New Hampshire Test is still utilized [Quen, 1978].) In the 1954 case, Judge David Bazelon, in Washington, D. C., changed the test of criminal responsibility for that district from the M'Naughten Rules to the Durham Rule, which states that a person is not criminally responsible if, at the time of the crime, her behavior was a "product" of her mental illness. Here, the statement was not a jury issue, but one for the psychiatrist; during the course of the next 18 years, under various modifications, the mental health expert was first told that he need not testify to the ultimate question and later told that he *must* not, because that would usurp the functions of the jury. Due to such confusion, the Durham Rule finally was discarded in 1972 and replaced with the Brawner decision (*U.S.* v. *Brawner,* 1972), which incorporates the American Law Institute Model Penal Code (1962) of criminal responsibility. This is the most recent and perhaps most respected test of criminal responsibility and has been adopted by most of the federal jurisdictions and by a number of states.

The American Law Insitutute Model Penal Code attempts to utilize current theories of psychodynamics, as well as the structure of previous tests of responsibility. The rule is that the defendant will be found not guilty by reason of insanity if he is suffering from mental illness at the time of the act, such that he lacked substantial capacity either to appreciate the criminality of his behavior or to conform his conduct to the requirements of law. In this test the purely cognitive notion of M'Naughten is replaced with the more comprehensive current view of individual psychology, combining the functions of cognition, volition, and conation. There have been other attempts at modifying the substance of the insanity rules, but it is primarily the M'Naughten Test and the ALI Penal Code that are used throughout the United States.

Disposition and Treatment of the
Criminally Insane

With respect to disposition of the individual found not guilty by reason of insanity, history has revealed that, in England, most such unfortunates have spent their days in Bedlam at the Queen's pleasure, which has meant until the end of their lives. In the United States they have spent decades at state hospitals for the criminally insane. It is only recently that several modifications of the law have altered significantly the disposition and treatment of those individuals found not guilty by reason of insanity.

If a defendant would spend the rest of his life in a hospital, then it would not make sense for him to have his defense counsel plead him insane unless he were trying to avoid the death penalty. Such, indeed, was the case for the first half of this century in the United States. Very few cases of insanity defense were brought, and even fewer were found to be valid by the court. However, since the rise of community mental health centers, the modification of commitment statutes, and the evolution of treatment modalities that make use of medication, all of which have improved the status of the mentally ill, changes have occurred, even in the treatment and disposition of those considered not guilty by reason of insanity (NGRI). No longer do NGRI patients stay in the hospital indefinitely, but many emerge within months or years after initial confinement. This change naturally has proved of interest to defense counsel, who have utilized the insanity defense in cases other than homicide or capital cases.

A number of cases of insanity have been tried following the 1954 Durham decision (*U.S.* v. *Durham*, 1954), for several reasons. Durham opened the door to more complete testimony by psychiatrists as expert witnesses. Judge Bazelon stated that the expert, in testifying in criminal cases, should tell the court what she can about the patient, to give the jury an understanding of the means by which the defendant functions. Previously, the expert was limited to a conclusory statement of insanity without elaboration. Other jurisdictions followed suit and expanded the rules of evidence for psychiatric testimony to include issues of "heat of passion," diminished responsibility, and diagnostic considerations other than psychosis affecting the ability to form "specific intent." Thus, the role of the mental health professional in criminal legal matters has been expanded significantly in the past two decades.

A more recent consideration has been the concept of "guilty but mentally ill," which began in Michigan about 1976 and has spread to Illinois and Indiana and is being considered in Pennsylvania and other states. This alternative approach has been developed because the court is concerned about the individual who has been found not guilty by reason of mental illness and who may emerge to the street more rapidly due to the liberalization of the mental health laws. Under the "guilty but mentally ill" provision, the defendant may be found guilty and sent to the correctional system, rather than found not guilty and sent to the mental health system. If he is guilty but mentally ill, he requires treatment, which he may obtain either in the prison or the hospital, but he must return to the prison to serve out his sentence after his treatment is complete. In that way the state has the ability and the authority to hold onto the patient–defendant until his sentence has been served. The important consideration for guilty but mentally ill is that it does serve as an alternative to the insanity defense and may decrease the number of individuals who are found legally insane. It is especially important, in those jurisdictions contemplating adopting the guilty but mentally ill provision, that facilities and resources do in fact exist, both in the hospitals and in the state prisons, for implementing the act by providing adequate treatment for these defendants.

The important consideration at present is the treatment of those found not guilty by reason of insanity and the legal mechanisms for their return to society. Perhaps the most sophisticated set of rules exists in New Jersey, under the cases of *State* v. *Krol* (1975) and *State* v. *Fields* (1977). In these cases the person found not guilty by reason of insanity has the right to a hearing every six to twelve months, and the judge makes the decision about gradual release from maximum security confinement. The criteria include not only mental illness, but also the provision for predicting dangerousness. Here, as we have discussed elsewhere, the mental health expert runs into a difficult problem because of her inability to make such predictions accurately. She must give clinical guidelines of potential violent behavior under certain conditions that the judge then may evaluate to determine whether the defendant is dangerous. The judge has the option of several levels of confinement, ranging from maximum security to moderate security, to minimum security, open door, ground privileges, home visits, halfway houses, or outpatient treatment, until the patient is finally discharged from the court's jurisdiction.

Formerly, such discharge planning was made by the psychiatrist or the mental health team in the hospital. However, a number of people who had been found not guilty by reason of insanity and were later discharged from the hospital did either commit suicide or further violent acts. The hospital, in some cases, was sued for "prematurely" releasing the patient. It makes good sense, then, to allow the judge—who is the one who initially committed the patient to the hospital—to be the one to ultimately decide to discharge the patient back into society and assume the responsibility for that decision.

Perhaps one of the most significant cases affecting the plight of the mentally ill charged with crime is the case of *Jackson* v. *Indiana* (1972). In that case, a deaf mute was held to be incompetent to stand trial and was held indefinitely in a hospital in Indiana. There was no chance that he would ever recover from his congenital "illness" and become competent to stand trial. Therefore, it was likely he would stay in the hospital indefinitely. The Supreme Court of the United States felt that was unfair to Jackson and to all other defendants who were awaiting trial because of incompetency. Therefore, the Jackson case ruled that a defendant may not be kept indefinitely as incompetent. There must come a time when an evaluation is presented to the court stating whether the defendant is competent, and, if he is not, whether he will ever in the foreseeable future become competent to stand trial. If the opinion is that he will not, then the judge has the option of sending the patient from the maximum security hospital to a general psychiatric hospital for treatment and gradual release to the community. The charges are then suspended or dropped, and the patient ultimately may return to the community.

In addition to assessing competency and criminal responsibility, the mental health professional is asked to evaluate people who engage in bizarre, unusual, violent, or sexually offensive behavior. Invariably, in a case of arson or rape, the psychiatrist will be called to evaluate the motivation, intent, psychodynamics, and state of mind of the individual committing such acts of passion or violence.

Juvenile Delinquency

The expert also may be called when juveniles commit criminal acts, especially if there is a question about certifying the juvenile as an adult to stand trial for a serious crime. Accused youngsters may not be required to stand trial as an adult for a crime if they are under the age of 13 or 14, the age varying by jurisdictions. (In most jurisdictions, though, the child will be adjudicated or heard by a juvenile court.) Between the ages of 14 and 18, they are considered to be juveniles and may be tried either as juveniles or as adults. They will be certified as adults if it can be shown at a hearing that these youngsters have not profited from experience, have a chronic pattern of antisocial behavior, and represent a significant danger to the community. Another criterion involves their ability to be rehabilitated by the age of 21.

The overlapping years of 18 to 21 are not explained clearly in the criminal law; that is, youngsters may not be tried as juveniles if they commit a crime when they are 18 or over, but they may be kept in juvenile facilities until the age of 21. It is often very difficult to make a determination about a person's potential for recovery by the age of 21, especially if he has a pattern of antisocial behavior. If he is easily led, mentally retarded, or becomes involved in a single episode of violence before the age of 18, it may be possible to place him in a special treatment program for juveniles and rehabilitate him successfully before the age of 21. If he is psychotic or significantly mentally ill at the time of the offense, then he may likely go to a hospital for treatment with the indication that his behavior was a product of his mental illness. The rationale is that, if the illness is successfully treated, he will not subsequently become violent or dangerous to the community.

Perhaps one of the more important areas of juvenile criminal matters is not the assessment for certification as a juvenile or as an adult, but the treatment of the juvenile offender. Many have been locked away in adult prisons for lack of juvenile facilities, and others are placed in very sophisticated, well-staffed juvenile treatment and rehabilitative programs. Some states have delineated various institutions for juveniles, for young adults, and for young offenders. There are also separate facilities for females in many jurisdictions. Most youngsters involved in criminal activities are placed on probation, and many commit subsequent crimes and become repeat offenders. The repeat offenders then ultimately end up in prison and later become adult offenders. The purpose of the juvenile system is to prevent this graduation to the more serious adult offenses; sometimes the efforts are successful, but often they are not.

Increasingly, social workers and child and adolescent psychiatrists and psychologists are becoming involved in forensic issues and in the treatment programs for youthful offenders. Primarily, youngsters become involved in violations of sexual and drug laws and become involved in alcoholism, burglary, larceny, and, occasionally, armed robbery and homicide. Most of the homicides juveniles commit involve family members, gang-related incidents, or close friends. Special consideration is given to those who commit parricide, that is, who kill their parents, and those who kill siblings. Teenage mothers are sometimes charged in the deaths of their newborn infants.

Sexual Offenders

Sexual offenders may be treated as special offenders in some jurisdictions (Sadoff, 1967). There has been, since 1937, a category of laws called the "sexual psychopath statutes." These statutes were created primarily to isolate the repetitive violent sexual offenders and give them special treatment within the criminal justice system. The intention was to see them as ill, rather than as evil, and to treat them, rather than punish them.

In some jurisdictions the special sexual offender statutes have been declared unconstitutional and special treatment has not been afforded. One of the concerns has been the indefinite or indeterminate sentence given to the sexual offender, which could run longer than the usual fixed sentence if he were convicted under the regular statute. Another concern has been the labeling of sex offenders as different from other offenders. A third concern has been the lumping together of sex offenders to give them similar treatment, when in fact there is as much difference between an exhibitionist and a rapist as there is between a thief and a murderer.

Some states, such as New Jersey, have very sophisticated sexual offender treatment facilities, which provide group and individual psychotherapy and medication during confinement, until a person is ready to receive gradual discharge into the community. A person is evaluated by a team of experts to determine if he is a "sexual psychopath," that is, a mentally disordered sex offender. If indeed he is a repetitive sex offender whose behavior illustrates his difficulty with controls and problems with impulses, then he will be recommended for treatment as a mentally disordered sex offender. He does receive an indefinite sentence and will be released only when he is considered to be improved sufficiently not to represent a threat to the community (Sadoff, 1977).

In Michigan, there was a consideration of conducting surgery on or giving hormonal treatment to those violent sex offenders who were sentenced to an indefinite term. The surgery consisted of an amygdalectomy: removing a piece of the brain to decrease the potential for violent sexual behavior. The study was to contrast and compare that type of treatment with the anti-androgen hormonal treatment, to determine their relative effectiveness. The study was curtailed under the Kaimowitz case (*Kaimowitz* v. *Michigan*, 1973), which stated that the patient had limited ability to give informed consent under the provisions of his indeterminate confinement.

For the very violent sex offenders, castration is used in some places outside the United States but has not been utilized recently in America. The antiandrogen hormonal treatment has been utilized effectively for some who are unable to control their violent sexual impulses. This treatment decreases generally the level of sexual interest and activity and is not specific for the particular offense for which the person has been charged. Other medications, such as psychotropic medicine for the psychotic sex offender who commits his bizarre sexual crimes as a result of his psychotic illness, also have been utilized successfully. For less violent sex offenders, group psychotherapy has been found helpful for persons placed on probation (Sadoff, 1976).

This author (Sadoff, 1972) previously has classified sex offenders into two major groups: the *aggressive* sex offenders and the *anonymous* sex offenders. The aggressive sex offenders include rapists, those who commit indecent sexual assaults, lust murderers, and necrophilics. Some forms of pedophilia are also assaultive and violent. The anonymous sex offenders appear to form a sort of continuum. They include the *frotteur*, who brushes up against women in crowded subways, buses, and elevators, touches private parts, and then runs away. At the next level is the exhibitionist, who exposes himself to a woman but does not become involved with her. Next is the voyeur, who looks in windows at others performing sex acts but does not become involved in sexual behavior except onanistically. Then comes the obscene telephone caller, the obscene letter writer, and finally the fetishist, one who obtains sexual gratification from inanimate objects representing the desired person. These people get arrested and become offenders when they steal objects of their fetish from others. The objects may include silk stockings, fur, underpants, and brassieres. All of these offenders are classified as anonymous because they are not directly involved with the object of their sexual interest and usually hide behind the telephone, writing instruments, or windows.

There is some concern that the minor sex offenders may progress to become major sex offenders. The analogy is similar to that of the user of marijuana progressing to heroin. A number of heroin users have started with marijuana, but the vast majority of marijuana smokers do not become heroin addicts. In the same way, some rapists may have a history of minor sex offenses, such as exhibitionism or voyeurism, but most exhibitionists and voyeurs do not progress to become rapists. It is important to note that each type of sex offender has a particular psychodynamic need that requires gratification. Other forms of sexual behavior may not be as gratifying.

Other Behavior Categories

The mental health professional also may be consulted in cases of arson, mutilation of bodies, and wanton destruction of property. Sometimes the examiner is called upon to judge in a deductive as well as inductive fashion. There may be a series of crimes for which there is no suspect, and the psychiatrist or psychologist may be called by the police or the prosecution to give a profile of the type of individual who may be involved in such behavior, based on her experience and based on the evidence developed by the police. In all of these matters it is important for the forensic mental health expert to be able to work closely with the coroner's office, forensic pathologists, and other forensic scientists engaged in the determination of scientific evidence in criminal matters.

Summary

Thus it is clear that the mental health professional involved in criminal matters goes way beyond the traditional treatment and diagnostic issues involved generally in mental health practice. He becomes a consultant to a number of agencies and must have a clear understanding of the criminal law and scientific evidence, as well as his own field of mental health expertise and the atmosphere within prisons and jails.

References

American Law Insitute Model Penal Code. Section 4.01, p. 66, Official Draft, May 4, 1962, Philadelphia.

Davis v. United States. 165 U.S. 373, 1897 (Irresistible Impulse Test).

Jackson v. Indiana. 406 U.S. 715, 1972.

Kaimowitz v. Michigan Department of Mental Health. Circuit Court, Wayne County, Michigan, 1973.

M'Naughten Rules 10 Clark and Finney 200, 8 English Reporter 718 (H. L.), 1843.

Quen, J. M. A History of the Anglo American Legal Psychiatry of Violence and Responsibility. In Robert Sadoff (Ed.), *Violence and Responsibility: The Individual, the Family and Society*. New York: SP Medical and Scientific Books, 1978.

Sadoff, R. L. Sexually Deviated Offenders. *Temple Law Quarterly, 40;* Spring/Summer 1967, 305–315.

Sadoff, R. L. Anonymous Sex Offenders, Medical Aspects of Human Sexuality, *Medical Aspects of Human Sexuality,* New York: Hospital Publications, Incorporated, 1972, 37–39.

Sadoff, R. L. Treatment of Violent Sex Offenders. *International Journal of Offender Therapy and Comparative Criminology, 20,* 1976, 75–80.

Sadoff, R. L. The Psychiatrist and the Rapist: Legal Issues. In R. T. Rada (Ed.), *Clinical Aspects of the Rapist.* New York: Grune & Stratton, 1977.

State v. Fields. 75 N.J. 588 A. 2d (Superior Court), 1977.

State v. Jones. 50 N.H. 369, 398, 9 Am. R. 242–264, 1871.

State v. Kroll. 68 N.J. 236, 344 A. 2d 289 (Superior Court), 1975.

State v. Pike. 49 N.H. 399, 6 Am. R. 533, 1869.

U.S. v. Brawner. 471 F. 2d 969, 1972.

U.S. v. Durham. 214 F. 2d 862, 1954.

Whitlock, F. A. *Criminal Responsibility and Mental Illness.* London: Butterworths, 1963, 13–15.

PART III

A Brief
Look into the
Future

Chapter 13

Epilogue

The proliferation of legal issues in the care and treatment of psychiatric patients has been so rapid that, once the issue is written about or discussed, it is almost obsolete because changes occur between the initial writing and the final publication. This is especially true in the area of mental health law, involving patients' rights and involuntary hospitalization, but it also concerns the traditional legal issues in which psychiatrists and other mental health professionals play a role. The changes will continue and the involvement intensify in personal-injury matters, in family disputes, and in the criminal law.

This book has attempted to summarize the major areas of legal concern for mental health professionals who treat the mentally ill. Primarily, it serves as a guide to the changes that have occurred, affecting the practice of the mental health professional. Its other purpose is to document the areas where the clinician's involvement intersects with the law. These areas of intersection have grown significantly in scope and intensity during the past several years.

We have come a long way in a relatively short time. Changes that have occurred that clinicians take for granted would not have been considered viable two decades ago. Patients' rights have assumed a significance that would not have been anticipated by clinicians practicing in the 1940s and 1950s. In many ways, the changes that have improved the lot of the psychiatric patient also have been beneficial to the clinician, whose work has become more highly structured and more precise, despite the greater scrutiny given by outside agencies. It is certainly more anxiety provoking and sometimes more agonizing to realize so clearly how ineffective some of our treatment methods are and how intractable some mental illnesses continue to be. The regulations have forced us to look more carefully at our treatment methods and apply them with greater specificity than we had in the past.

The changes will continue, and they will involve outpatients as well as hospitalized individuals. Rights of patients in the community have begun to emerge as a significant issue in the law, regulating the treatment of outpatients. Principles of law have been developed for community mental health centers, and the National Institute of Mental Health has sponsored attempts to develop a model teaching program of forensic principles to community mental health centers. The wave of the future lies in the community. As the changes were noted initially in hospitals and other institutions, they now must be implemented for patients in clinics, halfway houses, and community residential treatment centers. Thus it is especially important for the clinician to become increasingly familiar with the law and to learn the principles and guidelines that have been developed as they will apply to all patients. Increasingly, psychiatric patients will achieve greater autonomy, and the gap will widen between the competent, nondangerous patients treated in the community and those who are committed to hospitals as dangerous to self or others. Competency to make decisions about treatment and ability to control behavior will continue to determine treatment modalities.

Training Programs and Organizations in Forensic Sciences

Training programs in forensic psychiatry and other mental health professions also have proliferated and become more formalized in the past two decades. In the 1960s, forensic psychiatrists either were self-taught, learned from on-the-job experiences, or received tutorial training from a recognized forensic psychiatrist. More recently, the National Institute of Mental Health has sponsored various training programs, usually affiliated with criminal or correctional facilities, and other generalized training programs in forensic psychiatry have included experiences in civil law as well as in criminal procedures. The need for further training and more formalized education in the field led to the development of the American Academy of Psychiatry and the Law in 1968 and to the establishment of the American Law–Psychology Society at about the same time. The growth of these two organizations reflects the growing interest in the field and the need for further development.

As an example, the American Academy of Psychiatry and the Law began with eight individuals dedicated to the achievement of high-quality teaching of forensic psychiatry to medical students, residents, and fellows. Currently, the organization numbers over 800 members. In 1978, the American Board of Forensic Psychiatry issued its first certificates to diplomates who had successfully passed written and oral examinations. Similarly, the American Board of Forensic Psychology has certified many forensic psychologists. The growth of this interdisciplinary field also is reflected in the many books that have been written and published in law and nursing, law and social work, law and psychology, and law and psychiatry.

Standards of training in legal psychiatry have continued to develop, especially in the matters of faculty, curriculum, research, and clinical experiences. In addition to the specific organizations devoted to law and psychiatry,

or law and psychology, there exist two other major national organizat
need mention. The American Academy of Forensic Sciences has a se
psychiatry, numbering about 100 individuals, that is concerned abou
dards of training in legal psychiatry and in integration of principles of fo₁ensic
psychiatry with such other forensic sciences as criminalistics, questioned
documents, and jurisprudence. The American College of Legal Medicine, an
organization composed primarily of members who have both a medical and a
law degree, is concerned with the promotion of forensic psychiatry within the
field of legal medicine. This includes the integration of legal–psychiatric
principles in personal-injury matters, malpractice issues, and criminal matters, especially involving forensic pathology.

Ethical Considerations in Forensic Sciences

The important issues currently discussed by the members of professional
organizations devoted to law and mental health include the definition and
determination of dangerousness and the problems inherent in patients'
rights, especially the right to refuse mental health treatment. Primarily,
however, mental health professionals continue to look to ethical issues that
regulate the practice of forensic mental health. When should a sound principle become an ethical one? Under what circumstances should poor judgment
be formally distinguished and ethically prohibited in the field of legal
psychiatry or legal psychology?

Courts have become increasingly dependent upon forensic sciences in
aiding in the pursuit of justice. This dependency will continue, and the fields
of forensic science, forensic medicine, and law and mental health will continue to grow and become increasingly influential in courtroom work. For this
reason, it is essential for standards of training and quality of practice to be at
the highest level. As the court's dependency on these skills grows, so will the
degree of its scrutiny and regulation of them. Scientists, clinicians, practitioners, and physicians all must continue to develop, improve, and integrate their
skills to present the highest quality of work to the courts, which depend upon
professionals' findings, principles, and expertise.

Truly, there is an interdependence among medical and scientific professionals that, if properly developed, will provide much-needed help for judges
and lawyers in their work with their clients and these professionals' patients.

Appendix

Suggested Readings

General Texts

Law and Psychiatry

Allen, R. C., Ferster, E. Z., & Rubin, J. G. *Readings in Law and Psychiatry*. Rev. and exp. ed. Baltimore, Md.: The Johns Hopkins University Press, 1975.

Bromberg, W. *The Uses of Psychiatry in the Law: A Clinical View of Forensic Psychiatry*. Westport, Conn.: Quorum Books, 1979.

Brooks, A. D. *Law, Psychiatry, and the Mental Health System*. Boston: Little, Brown, 1974; with 1980 suppl.

Curran, W. J., McGarry, A. L., & Petty, C. S. *Modern Legal Medicine, Psychiatry, and Forensic Science*. Philadelphia: F. A. Davis, 1980.

Davidson, H. *Forensic Psychiatry*. 2d ed. New York: Ronald Press, 1965.

Guttmacher, M. S. *The Role of Psychiatry in Law*. Springfield, Ill.: Charles C Thomas, 1968.

Guttmacher, M. S., and Weihofen, H. *Psychiatry and the Law*. New York: W. W. Norton, 1952.

Halleck, S. L. *Law in the Practice of Psychiatry: A Handbook for Clinicians*. New York: Plenum Medical Book Co., 1980.

Hofling, C. K. *Law and Ethics in the Practice of Psychiatry*. New York: Bruner-Mazel, 1980.

Katz, J., Goldstein, J., & Dershowitz, A. M. *Psychoanalysis, Psychiatry and the Law*. New York: Free Press, 1967.

Overholser, W. *The Psychiatrist and the Law*. New York: Harcourt Brace, 1953.

Robitscher, J. B. *Pursuit of Agreement, Psychiatry and the Law*. Philadelphia: Lippincott, 1966.

Sadoff, R. L. *Forensic Psychiatry: A Practical Guide for Lawyers and Psychiatrists*. Springfield, Ill.: Charles C Thomas, 1975.

Slovenko, R. *Psychiatry and Law*. Boston: Little, Brown, 1973.

Law and Psychology

Cooke, G. *The Role of the Forensic Psychologist*. Springfield, Ill.: Charles C Thomas, 1980.

Sales, B. D. *Psychology in the Legal Process*. New York: Spectrum, 1980.

Schwitzgebel, R. L., & Schwitzgebel, R. K. *Law and Psychological Practice*. New York: John Wiley, 1980.

Law and Mental Health

Barton, W. E., & Sanborn, C. J. *Law and the Mental Health Professions: Friction at the Interface*. New York: International University Press, 1978.

Brakel, S. J., & Rock, R. S. *The Mentally Disabled and the Law*. Rev. ed. Chicago: University of Chicago Press, 1971.

Stone, A. A. *Mental Health and Law: A System in Transition*. Washington, D.C.: National Institute of Mental Health, 1975.

Law and Nursing

Cazalas, M. W. *Nursing and the Law*. Germantown, Md.: Aspen Systems, 1978.

Specialized Texts in Law and Mental Health and Law and Psychiatry

Involuntary Commitment and Patients' Rights

Asch, S. H. *Mental Disability in Civil Practice*. Rochester, N.Y.: The Lawyers Cooperative, 1973.

Kittrie, N. *The Right to Be Different*. Baltimore: Johns Hopkins University Press, 1971.

Morris, G. H. *The Mentally Ill and the Right to Treatment*. Springfield, Ill.: Charles C Thomas, 1970.

Peszke, M. *Involuntary Treatment of the Mentally Ill*. Springfield, Ill.: Charles C Thomas, 1975.

Roth, L. H. A Commitment Law for Patients, Doctors, and Lawyers. *American Journal of Psychiatry, 136*, 1979, 1121–1127.

Slovenko, R. *Psychotherapy, Confidentiality and Privileged Communication*. Springfield, Ill.: Charles C Thomas, 1966.

Szasz, T. *Law, Liberty and Psychiatry*. New York: Macmillan, 1963.

Child Psychiatry and the Law

Goldstein, J., Freud, A., & Solnit, A. J. *Beyond the Best Interests of the Child*. New York: The Free Press, 1973.

Schetky, D. J., & Benedek, E. P. *Child Psychiatry and the Law*. New York: Bruner-Mazel, 1980.

Stuart, I. R., & Abt, L. E. *Children of Separation and Divorce: Management and Treatment*. New York: Van Nostrand Reinhold, 1981.

Personal-Injury Matters

Keiser, L. *The Traumatic Neurosis*. Philadelphia: Lippincott, 1968.

Lewis, M., & Sadoff, R. L. *Psychic Injuries*. Vol. 12, Courtroom Medicine Series. New York: Matthew Bender, 1975.

Criminal Law and Mental Illness

Fingarette, H., & Hasse, A. F. *Mental Disabilities and Criminal Responsibility*. Berkeley, Calif.: University of California Press, 1979.

Goldstein, A. S. *The Insanity Defense*. New Haven, Conn.: Yale University Press, 1967.

Group for the Advancement of Psychiatry. Pamplet entitled Misuse of Psychiatry in the Criminal Courts: Competency to Stand Trial. Vol. 8, Report 89. New York, February 1974.

Guttmacher, M. S. *The Mind of the Murderer*. New York: Farrar, Strause, and Cudahy, 1960.

Halleck, S. L. *Psychiatry and the Dilemmas of Crime*. New York: Harper & Row, 1967.

Halleck, S. L., & Bromberg, W. *Psychiatric Aspects of Criminology*. Springfield, Ill.: Charles C Thomas, 1968.

MacDonald, D. *Psychiatry and the Criminal*. 2nd ed. Springfield, Ill.: Charles C Thomas, 1969.

National Institute of Mental Health. Pamphlet entitled Competency to Stand Trial and Mental Illness. Rockville, Md.: NIMH, 1973.

Roche, P. Q. *The Criminal Mind*. New York: Farrar, Strause, and Cudahy, 1958.

Slovenko, R. *Crime, Law and Corrections*. Springfield, Ill.: Charles C Thomas, 1966.

Steadman, H. *Beating a Rap? Defendants Found Incompetent to Stand Trial*. Chicago: The University of Chicago Press, 1979.

Weihofen, H. *The Urge to Punish*. New York: Farrar, Strause, and Cudahy, 1956.

Whitlock, F. A. *Criminal Responsibility and Mental Illness*. London: Butterworth's, 1963.

Zilboorg, G. *The Psychology of the Criminal Act and Punishment*. New York: Harcourt Brace, 1954.

Sex Offenders and Mental Illness

Karpman, B. *The Sexual Offender and His Offenses*. New York: Julian Press, 1954.

Rada, R. T. *Clinical Aspects of the Rapist*. New York: Grune & Stratton, 1978.

Resnick, H. L. P., & Wolfgang, M. E. *Sexual Behaviors: Social, Clinical, and Legal Aspects*. Boston: Little, Brown, 1972.

Slovenko, R. *Sexual Behavior and the Law*. Springfield, Ill.: Charles C Thomas, 1965.

Violence and Dangerousness

American Psychiatric Association. Task Force Report 8: Clinical Aspects of the Violent Individual. Washington, D.C.: APA, 1974.

Monahan, J. *The Clinical Prediction of Violent Behavior*. Rockville, Md.: National Institute of Mental Health, 1981.

Rappeport, J. R. *The Clinical Evaluation of the Dangerousness of the Mentally Ill*. Springfield, Ill.: Charles C Thomas, 1967.

Sadoff. R. L. *Violence and Responsibility*. New York: Spectrum, 1978.

Malpractice Considerations

Cohen, R. J. *Malpractice, A Guide for Mental Health Professionals*. New York: Free Press, 1979.

Dawidoff, D. J. *The Malpractice of Psychiatrists*. Springfield, Ill.: Charles C Thomas, 1973.

Miscellaneous Texts

Rheinstein, M. *Marriage Stability, Divorce, and the Law*. Chicago: Univeristy of Chicago Press, 1972.

Robitscher, J. *The Powers of Psychiatry*. Boston: Houghton Mifflin, 1980.

Ziskin, J. *Coping with Psychiatric and Psychological Testimony*. 2nd ed. Beverly Hills, Calif.: Law and Psychology Press, 1970.

Index

Index